# VIGILANCE AND SELF-EXAMINATION

*Kitāb al-murāqaba wa'l-muḥāsaba*

BOOK XXXVIII of
THE REVIVAL OF THE RELIGIOUS SCIENCES
*Iḥyā' ʿulūm al-dīn*

OTHER TITLES IN THE ISLAMIC TEXTS SOCIETY
AL-GHAZĀLĪ SERIES

FROM THE *Iḥyāʾ ʿulūm al-dīn*

Al-Ghazālī on Invocations & Supplications

Al-Ghazālī on the Manners Relating to Eating

Al-Ghazālī on the Lawful & the Unlawful

Al-Ghazālī on Conduct in Travel

Al-Ghazālī on Disciplining the Soul & Breaking the Two Desires

Al-Ghazālī on Patience & Thankfulness

Al-Ghazālī on Love, Longing, Intimacy & Contentment

Al-Ghazālī on Intention, Sincerity & Truthfulness

Al-Ghazālī on the Remembrance of Death & the Afterlife

OTHER WORKS

Al-Ghazālī on the Ninety-Nine Beautiful Names of God
(*al-Maqṣad al-asnā fī sharḥ asmāʾ Allāh al-ḥusnā*)

Al-Ghazālī Letter to a Disciple
(*Ayyuhāʾl-walad*)

# AL-GHAZĀLĪ

# ON VIGILANCE & SELF-EXAMINATION

*Kitāb al-murāqaba · wa'l-muḥāsaba ·*

BOOK XXXVIII of THE REVIVAL OF THE RELIGIOUS SCIENCES

*Iḥyā' ʿulūm al-dīn* · translated with notes by ANTHONY F. SHAKER

This first edition published 2015 by
THE ISLAMIC TEXTS SOCIETY
MILLER'S HOUSE
KINGS MILL LANE
GREAT SHELFORD
CAMBRIDGE CB22 5EN, U.K.

Reprint 2016

British Library Cataloguing-in-Publication Data.
A catalogue record for this book is
available from the British Library.

ISBN: 978 1903682 326 cloth
ISBN: 978 1903682 333 paper

# CONTENTS

Al-Ghazālī's Introduction to the
*Revival of the Religious Sciences* VII

Publisher's Introduction XVII

## THE BOOK OF VIGILANCE AND SELF-EXAMINATION

[Prologue 1]

CHAPTER ONE: The First Station of Steadfast Commitment: Agreeing Upon the Conditions 5

CHAPTER TWO: The Second Steadfast Commitment: Vigilance 13

CHAPTER THREE: The Third Steadfast Commitment: Self-examination After the Act 33

CHAPTER FOUR: The Fourth Steadfast Commitment: Punishing the Soul for Its Dereliction 39

CHAPTER FIVE: The Fifth Steadfast Commitment: Renewed Striving 44

CHAPTER SIX: The Sixth Steadfast Commitment: Self-reproach and Self-censure 68

Notes 85
Appendix: Persons Cited in Text 93
Bibliography 105
Index to Qur'ānic Quotations 109
General Index 111

# Al-Ghazālī's Introduction to the *Revival of the Religious Sciences*

*The importance of Imam Ghazālī's Introduction to the* Revival of the Religious Sciences *cannot be overstated; it outlines the reasons and motives for the writing of the* Revival *and it explains the structure of the work as a whole. The Islamic Texts Society has decided to include this Introduction at the beginning of all its translations from the* Revival, *including in revised editions of earlier translations. In the list of the forty chapters below, the choice of translation for the titles of the not-yet-published chapters is not restrictive; the final translations will be left to the individual translators and the list below will be periodically updated with the latest chapter headings.*

In the Name of God, the Compassionate, the Merciful

FIRSTLY, I PRAISE GOD with many continuous praises; though the praise of those who praise is meagre in front of what is due to His majesty.

Secondly, I invoke blessings and peace upon His Messenger—blessings that encompass along with the leader of mankind (*sayyid al-bashar*)[A] all other prophets.

Thirdly, I ask for His guidance (Gloried and Exalted is He) as I resolve to write a book for the revival of the religious sciences.

Fourthly, I hasten to put a stop to your censure O critic who—among those who reject [what we say]—has gone to extremes in his criticism, and who—among those who deny [us] and are heedless—is immoderate in his chiding and rejection.[B]

[A] The Prophet Muḥammad.

[B] It is not clear if Ghazālī had a particular person in mind when he penned

My tongue has been set loose, and the responsibility to speak out and to discourse have become incumbent on me due to your persistent blindness to the obvious truth, your obstinacy in backing falsehood and in embellishing ignorance, and your stirring up hostility against him who has given preference to stepping somewhat aside from social conventions and who has verged slightly from formality. [He does this] for the sake of acting according to the dictates of knowledge and in eagerness to gain what God (Great and Glorious is He) has commanded in purifying the soul and rectifying the heart, thus somewhat redeeming a life wasted and in the hope of escaping complete rack and ruin. Hence, he seeks to avoid the risk of being associated with those about whom the Law giver (may God bless him and grant him peace) has said, 'The one who will be most severely punished on the Day of Judgement is he who was granted knowledge (*ᶜālim*)[A] and whom God (glory be to Him) did not make benefit from his knowledge.'[B]

By my life, there is no reason for the persistence of your opposition except for the malady that has encompassed the vast majority—indeed the multitudes. [The malady of] the inability to discern the weight of the matter, the ignorance of how grave the situation is and how crucial the issue, that the Hereafter is approaching and that this life is departing, that the end of life is near and the journey still far, that the provision is scanty and the danger immense, that the way is blocked, that for the discerning critic the knowledge and the acts that are purely for God are what avail, and that to pursue the path of the Hereafter—with all its many dangers and without a guide or companion—is exhausting and arduous.

this very severe and direct criticism here and below. Its personal nature does suggest that he did have someone in mind, but he could equally have used this form as a general accusation against a specific group.

[A] The term *ᶜālim* (pl. *ᶜulamā'*) has been translated both as 'he who has been granted or who possesses knowledge' and as 'scholar' according to the context.

[B] Ṭabarānī, *al-Muᶜjam al-ṣaghīr*, 1.182.

The guides of the way are those who possess knowledge (*ʿulamāʾ*) who are the heirs of the prophets.[A] This age is devoid of them and those who remain are impersonators; most have been overpowered by the devil and been led astray by iniquity. Each one is engrossed with his earthly gain; he sees what is right objectionable and what is objectionable right; thus the banner of religion has been pulled down and the beacon of guidance all over the world is extinguished.

[These impersonators] deceive people into thinking that knowledge is only decrees of the state (*fatāwā ḥukūma*) that judges use in order to resolve disputes when there is disturbance by the rabble, or a form of debating which a person seeking to show off equips himself with in order to gain superiority and the upper hand, or ornate language which a preacher uses to lure in the common people. These three [means] are all they could find to snare illegal gain and to net the vanities [of the world].

Now the knowledge of the path to the Hereafter (*ʿilm ṭarīq al-ākhira*)—which was followed by the pious predecessors and which was called by God (Glorified is He) in His Book: law (*fiqh*), wisdom (*ḥikma*), knowledge (*ʿilm*), luminescence (*ḍiyāʾ*), light (*nūr*), guidance (*hidāya*), right-direction (*rushd*)—has become among people a thing hidden and forgotten.

As this [situation] is a calamitous fissure in religion and as the times are dark, I concluded that it is crucial to undertake the composition of this book in order to revive the religious sciences, to seek out the methods of the previous leaders [of religion], and to clarify what the prophets and the pious predecessors considered beneficial knowledge (may God grant them all peace).

I divided it into four quarters: the Quarter of the Acts of Worship (*rubʿ al-ʿibādāt*), the Quarter of the Norms of Daily Life (*rubʿ al-ʿādāt*), the Quarter of the Moral Vices (*rubʿ al-muhlikāt*) and the Quarter of the Saving Virtues (*rubʿ al-munjiyāt*).

[A] ʿIrāqī, I.6 says this is in Abū Dāʾūd, Tirmidhī, Ibn Māja and in *Ṣaḥīḥ* Ibn Ḥibbān on the authority of Abū al-Dardāʾ.

I began the whole [of the work] with 'The Book of Knowledge'[A] (*Kitāb al-ʿilm*) because [knowledge] is of the utmost importance. Firstly, I reveal the knowledge that God (Great and Glorious is He) ordered the elite (*aʿyān*) to seek in the words of His Prophet (may God bless him and grant him peace) when he said, 'Seeking knowledge is a legal obligation (*farīḍa*) for every Muslim';[B] then, I differentiate [in the book] between knowledge that is beneficial and [knowledge] that is harmful, for may God bless him and grant him peace said, 'We seek refuge in You from knowledge that does not benefit';[C] and I illustrate how far the people of this age have departed from right conduct, and how deceived they are by glossy illusions[D] and by their contentment with the husk rather than the kernel of knowledge.

The Quarter of the Acts of Worship is made up of ten Books:

1 The Book of Knowledge
2 The Book of the Foundations of the Articles of Faith
3 The Book of the Mysteries of Purity
4 The Book of the Mysteries of the Prayer
5 The Book of the Mysteries of Almsgiving
6 The Book of the Mysteries of Fasting
7 The Book of the Mysteries of the Pilgrimage
8 The Book of Ways of Reciting of the Qur'ān
9 The Book of Invocations and Supplications
10 The Book of Classification of Litanies and the Division of the Night Vigil

The Quarter of the Norms of Daily Life is made up of ten Books:

11 The Book of the Manners Related to Eating
12 The Book of Conduct in Marriage
13 The Book of Ways of Earning and Making a Living

[A] We have retained Book for the titles of the chapters of the *Revival*.
[B] Ibn Mājā 224.
[C] Muslim 2722.
[D] Lit. 'mirage' (*sarāb*).

14 The Book of the Lawful and the Unlawful
15 The Book of Ways of Friendship, Brotherhood and Companionship
16 The Book of Conduct in Seclusion
17 The Book of Conduct in Travel
18 The Book of Conduct in Audition and Ecstasy
19 The Book of Enjoining the Good and Prohibiting Evil
20 The Book of Conduct of Living and the Qualities of Prophethood

The Quarter of the Moral Vices is made up of ten Books:

21 The Book of Expounding the Wonders of the Heart
22 The Book of Disciplining the Soul
23 The Book of Breaking the Two Desires
24 The Book of the Vices of the Tongue
25 The Book of Condemnation of Anger, Rancour and Envy
26 The Book of Condemnation of the World
27 The Book of Condemnation of Avarice and Love of Wealth
28 The Book of Condemnation of Status and Ostentation
29 The Book of Condemnation of Pride and Conceit
30 The Book of Condemnation of Self-delusion

The Quarter of the Saving Virtues is made up of ten Books:

31 The Book of Repentance
32 The Book of Patience and Thankfulness
33 The Book of Fear and Hope
34 The Book of Poverty and Abstinence
35 The Book of Unity of God and Reliance upon Him
36 The Book of Love, Longing, Intimacy and Contentment
37 The Book of Intention, Truthfulness and Sincerity
38 The Book of Vigilance and Self-examination
39 The Book of Reflection
40 The Book of the Remembrance of Death and the Afterlife

As to the Quarter of the Acts of Worship, I mention in it the mysteries of their conduct, the subtleties of their ways, the secrets of their meanings, and what the practicing scholar (*al-ʿālim al-ʿāmil*) cannot do without; he would not be among the scholars of the Hereafter if he were not versed in these. Much of this has been neglected in the studies of jurisprudence.

In the Quarter of the Norms of Daily Life, I discuss the secrets of the [various] relations that take place between people (*muʿāmalāt*),[A] their deeper meanings, the subtleties of their ways, and the mysteries of the piety (*waraʿ*) that should run through them. [All] these are what no religious person (*mutadayyin*) can do without.

In the Quarter of the Moral Vices, I list every reprehensible character trait (*khuluq madhmūm*) that the Qur'ān commanded to be uprooted, and the soul to be cleansed and the heart to be purified thereof. I include for each of these character traits its definition (*ḥadd*) and its reality (*ḥaqīqa*), then the cause from which it derives, the evils that result from it, the signs by which it can be recognised, and the different remedies that can be used to eliminate it.

Accompanying all this are proofs from Qur'ānic verses, Prophetic reports (*akhbār*) and narratives (*āthār*).

As to the Quarter of the Saving Virtues, I mention every laudable character trait and every desirable quality of those near [to God] (*muqarrabūn*) and of the righteous (*ṣiddīqūn*) through which the servant can gain proximity to the Lord of the worlds. For every quality I give its definition and its reality, the means by which it can be attained, the fruits that are derived from it, the signs by which it can be recognised, the merits which make it desirable, and the ways that it has been affirmed by the Law (*sharʿ*) and by the intellect (*ʿaql*).

[A] The plural *muʿāmalāt* (sing. *muʿāmala*) does not have the same meaning as *ʿilm al-muʿāmala* below and therefore they have been translated differently according to Ghazālī's intention for each.

Other titles have been written about some of these topics,[A] but this [present] work is distinguished from them in five ways:

Firstly, it clarifies what is complicated in them and elucidates what they have mentioned in passing.

Secondly, it organises what is scattered in them and systematises what is disparate in them.

Thirdly, it summarises what they have overly discussed and gives precision to what they have affirmed.

Fourthly, it deletes what they have repeated and corroborates what they have formulated.

Fifthly, it clarifies ambiguous matters that are difficult to understand and that have never even been the subject of books. For though all [who write] may follow a single method, this does not preclude each one who pursues [this method] from paying special attention to a matter that concerns him and which his colleagues may not know about, or may be aware of it but overlooked it in writing, or may not have overlooked it but something caused them to turn away from it.

While it includes all the [above mentioned] sciences, these are the [five] specific attributes of this work.

Two things prompted me to compose this book in four quarters. The first and primary motive is that this arrangement is indispensable when researching and elaborating [on a subject], given that the knowledge by which we approach the Hereafter is divided into 'the knowledge of contingent actions' (*ʿilm al-muʿāmala*)[B] and 'direct knowledge' (*ʿilm al-mukāshafa*).[C]

[A] In writing the *Revival*, Ghazālī was fully aware of the religious literature of his time and, in the *Revival*, he both draws on a number of titles (for example, Makkī's *Qūt al-qulūb*) and takes this literature a step further.

[B] *Muʿāmala* (pl. *muʿāmalāt*) is usually translated as 'transaction', 'procedure', 'treatment'. But for Ghazālī, there is a return to the root of the term in *ʿamala*, 'to act'. In translating *ʿilm al-muʿāmala* as 'the knowledge of contingent actions', we have taken both Ghazālī's own definition and the root of the term into consideration.

[C] In Sufism, *mukāshafa* is a technical term meaning 'unveiling' and 'direct

By direct knowledge, I mean [the knowledge] whose only requirement is to reveal the object of knowledge (*maʿlūm*) and nothing else.

By the knowledge of contingent actions, I mean [the knowledge] of the actions that necessarily accompany direct knowledge.[A]

The aim of this book is exclusively the knowledge of contingent actions and not direct knowledge which—despite it being the goal of those who seek and the aspiration for the vision of the righteous—is beyond being documented in books. The knowledge of contingent actions is a means to it. The prophets (may God bless them and grant them peace) only spoke to people about the knowledge of the path (*ʿilm al-ṭarīq*) and about guidance to it. As to direct knowledge, they only mentioned it through symbol and allusion, and by way of comparison and in a general fashion, knowing that people's understanding falls short of comprehending it. Now, those who possess knowledge are the heirs of the prophets and thus they cannot verge from the method of emulating and imitating [the prophets].

Knowledge of contingent actions is divided into outer knowledge (*ʿilm ẓāhir*), by which I mean the knowledge of the actions for bodily parts; and inner knowledge (*ʿilm bāṭin*), by which I mean the knowledge of the actions of the heart.

or experiential knowledge'; it is linked with *dhawq* 'tasting'. The term has been translated as 'revelation' (Nabih Amin Faris, *The Book of Knowledge*, p. xiv), but it is clear from Ghazālī's definition that it is not revelation as *waḥy*, but is direct spiritual knowledge of immutable truths.

[A] It should not be understood from this very concise definition that Ghazālī intends each individual to act exclusively on his or her own direct knowledge. The actions referred to here are those derived from the Qurʾān, the *Sunna* of the Prophet, and the example of the pious predecessors and the saints; thus actions based in revelation and in the direct knowledge of the Prophet and the saintly. Each of the chapters of the *Revival* invariably starts with reference to Qurʾanic verses, the traditions of the Prophet and the narratives of the Companions and the saints, making them the example to be followed.

What applies to the bodily parts is either worship (*ʿibāda*) or norms of daily life (*ʿāda*).[A]

What occurs in the heart—which by dint of being veiled from the senses is part of the heavenly realm (*malakūt*)—is either commendable (*maḥmūd*) or reprehensible (*madhmūm*).[B]

Thus, this knowledge [of contingent actions] by necessity divides into two halves: outer and inner. The outer half, which is connected to the bodily parts, is itself divided into worship and norms of daily life; while the inner half, which is connected to the states of the heart and the attributes of the soul, is divided into either what is reprehensible or what is commendable. Therefore, the result is four parts and no examination of the knowledge of contingent actions can go beyond these divisions.

The secondary motive [for composing this book]: I have found that—[despite jurisprudence] being exploited by those who do not fear God to boast, and their making use of its prestige and standing in competing [with each other]—there is a genuine desire for knowledge on behalf of the students of jurisprudence. [Thus, in imitation of the works of jurisprudence,] it is divided into four quarters; for he who takes on the garb of the beloved becomes beloved. I believe that styling the book in the form of [books of] jurisprudence will gently lead hearts [to it]. This was the reason why one of those who wanted to draw the attention of persons in authority to [the science of] medicine structured it in the form of an astrological almanac, arranged it into tables and numbers, and called it 'The Almanac of Health', that their familiarity with this kind [of science] may draw them to reading [his title].

Gently leading hearts to the knowledge that benefits everlasting life is more important than leading them to medicine that

[A] Elaborated in the Quarter of Acts of Worship and the Quarter of Norms of Daily Life.

[B] Elaborated in the Quarter of the Moral Vices and the Quarter of the Saving Virtues.

only benefits the health of the body. The fruit of this knowledge is the health of hearts and souls and the arrival through it to life that never ends. How can the medicine that is used to heal bodies, necessarily destined before long to corruption, compare with this!

We ask God (glory be to Him) guidance to what is right and just, for He is the Generous, the Munificent.

The Islamic Texts Society
Rabīᶜ al-thanī 1436/February 2015

# PUBLISHER'S INTRODUCTION

*The Book of Vigilance and Self-Examination* (Kitāb al-murāqaba wa'l-muḥāsaba) is the thirty-eighth chapter of the *Revival of the Religious Sciences* and follows on from *The Book of Intention, Sincerity and Truthfulness*. In the latter chapter, Ghāzalī focused on intention, how to verify it and how to ensure its sincerity and truthfulness. *The Book of Vigilance and Self-examination* builds on this and concentrates on how to observe the soul and how to maintain its faithfulness to its Lord.

Yet, while the chapter is entitled 'Vigilance and Self-examination', neither are the goal. In his prologue, Ghazālī refers to the Qur'ān and states that God has enjoined upon creation patience (*ṣabr*)[A] and 'steadfast commitment' (*murābaṭa*), and that *murābaṭa* is made up of six stations: agreeing upon the conditions (*mushāraṭa*), vigilance (*murāqaba*), self-examination (*muḥāsaba*), punishment (*muʿāqaba*), renewed striving (*mujāhada*) and, finally, self-censure (*muʿātaba*).

The Arabic root of *murābaṭa* is *r-b-ṭ*; it carries the basic meaning of attaching or tying. It is connected with *ribāṭ*, the name for the small military fortifications of the early Islamic conquests, and literally means 'where cavalry horses are stationed'; *murābiṭūn* are those who are 'mounted or ready for battle'. For Ghazālī's purpose, *murābaṭa* is the struggle against the self (*jihād al-nafs*), and the *murābiṭ* is one who fights against his own self (*mujāhid nafsihi*). This echoes the early view of ʿAbd Allāh Ibn al-Mubārak (d. 180/797) who asserted that *ribāṭ* is 'the striving (*jihād*) against the self and

[A] See *Al-Ghazālī on Patience and Thankfulness*, trans. H. Littlejohn, Cambridge: Islamic Texts Society, 2011.

the passions (*mujāhadat al-nafs wa'l-hawā*)' because it refers to the 'greater *jihād*', which, he says, is 'the true *jihād* (*ḥaqq al-jihād*)' and alludes to the Prophet's saying, 'We returned from the lesser *jihād* to the greater *jihād*.'[A]

In *The Book of Vigilance and Self-examination*, the goal is 'steadfast commitment' (*murābaṭa*) in the struggle against the self (*jihād*), and the tools are divided into those that precede the act—agreeing upon the conditions (*mushāraṭa*); those that accompany the act—vigilance (*murāqaba*); and those that follow the act—self-examination (*muḥāsaba*), punishment (*muʿāqaba*), renewed striving (*mujāhada*) and self-censure (*muʿātaba*).

Thus one has to instruct the soul as to what it has to do and what it has to desist from. Once the terms are agreed, there has to be constant vigilance of the soul as it is untrustworthy and cannot be left to itself. Then the acts have to be examined to verify whether they have been true to the conditions. If the soul has not lived up to the conditions imposed upon it, then there is punishment. As a consequence, it is compelled to continue its striving and the intellect (*ʿaql*), which is its guide, continues to censure it in order to keep it on the straight and narrow.

In keeping with certain verses from the Qur'ān which speak of gaining Paradise or losing one's soul in terms of trade (Q.II.16, II.102, II.207, XXXV.29, IV.74), Ghazālī discusses the six stations of *murābaṭa* as a commercial transaction between the intellect and the soul in the way towards the Hereafter. In the first chapter, he says, 'Know that when those who engage in commerce and deal in commodities settle accounts, they seek a healthy profit. Hence, the trader avails himself of his associate, handing him money for the trade and then settling his account with him. It is the same with the intellect (*ʿaql*) as it does commerce on the way to the Hereafter. Its object and profit is the purification of the soul, because its felicity is through this...Now, as the other party can be adversarial, disputing and rivalling him for profit,

[A] Bayhaqī, *Kitāb al-zuhd*, vol. II.265, no. 373.

first, he needs to agree on the conditions; second, to be vigilant with him; third, to call him to account; and, fourth, to punish or censure him. By the same token, the intellect first needs to set the conditions for the soul (*mushāraṭat al-nafs*); then to assign tasks to it, lay down the conditions, guide it to the paths of felicity and force it to undertake such paths without for a single moment neglecting to keep vigilant over it. Whenever, on the other hand, the intellect neglects the soul, it will find nothing but disloyalty in it and the loss of capital—just like the disloyal servant who, left at liberty, may abscond with the money.'

In chapter two, Ghazālī gives the merits of vigilance through a long list of anecdotes and then he explains the reality of vigilance. Here he explains vigilance through two levels partly based on the division of people in Chapter LVI of the Qur'ān: the vigilance of the perfectly truthful among those near to God (*al-ṣiddīqūn min al-muqarrabūn*) and the vigilance of the pious (*wariʿūn*) among the people of the right hand. The discussion here is very close to that in *The Book of Intention, Sincerity and Truthfulness* as vigilance not only observes actions but also examines and verifies their motives. 'The first consideration for the vigilant person is to look into the matter of concern or the activity: Is it for God or for passion?... The second consideration is that of vigilance upon the initiation of action—namely, checking how the action [is executed] in compliance with the prerogative of God in the matter, improving the intention in order to complete and perfect the action, and pursuing it as far as possible.'

The chapter on vigilance is followed by that on self-examination. In this third chapter, Ghazālī says, 'Know that just as the servant of God has from the beginning of the day to obtain his soul's agreement with truthful admonition, so by day's end he has a time within which to demand an accounting and to examine his soul for all it has or has not done.'

Here again Ghazālī returns to the idea of transactions and trade, saying, 'The examination of an associate implies consideration of the capital, the profit and the loss in order to distinguish the surplus from the loss. If there is a gain in revenue, it is received in full and gratefully. In the event of a loss, it is claimed as a liability and assigned as a future indemnity. The same holds true for the capital of the worshipper with respect to his debt in obligations, his profit in supererogatory acts and virtues—his loss is disobedience.'

The remainder of the chapter is a series of anecdotes and examples of how to examine oneself. These anecdotes are, however, not an end in themselves. Ghazālī considered the time he was living in to be decadent and says that companionship of good people is hard to come by. In their absence, hearing about them and imitating their example is very instructive. Thus his purpose in this chapter, and in the next—on punishing the soul for its dereliction—which is almost entirely a series of anecdotes, is to provide what he considers as second-best to good companionship, namely, hearing about what the ancients did, perusing their reports with the aim of copying their example.

Chapter five on renewed striving is the longest of the six chapters. Here Ghazālī says that if a person finds his soul slothful and reluctant to turn to virtue and devotion, then he has to force it to do so. Ghazālī follows this by giving a long list of anecdotes about those who strived with their souls for the sake of God and the Hereafter including a number of anecdotes of women.

The final chapter is taken up with describing the different types of soul and how, through constant reproach and censure, the soul that incites to evil can be changed to the soul that is tranquil and pleasing to God. Ghazālī sets the example of how to speak to the soul and how to admonish it with a long section speaking directly to the soul addressing it again and again with 'Woe unto you. O soul' and ends it by saying, 'Following the example of Adam your Father, say [O soul], "O Most Merciful of the merciful, O Compassionate, O Granter of Mercy, O Gentle One, O Great One, O Kind One—I am the inveterate sinner, the reckless one who knows no abstinence, the profligate with no shame. This is the station of the humble petitioner, wretchedly poor and miserably weak, drowning and doomed. Hasten to my succour, give me repose, show me the effects of Your mercy. Let me taste the coolness of Your forgiveness. Bestow upon me the power of Your protection, O Most Merciful of the merciful.'"

# THE BOOK OF VIGILANCE AND SELF-EXAMINATION

Being the Eighth Book of the Quarter of Saving Virtues

## [PROLOGUE]

*In the Name of God, Most Compassionate and Merciful*

PRAISE BE TO GOD who grants every soul what it has earned; who watches every perpetrator of outrage,[1] who fathoms the innermost recesses of the hearts and best reckons the thoughts stirring inside his servants. Not an atom's weight in heaven and earth, whether in motion or rest, escapes His knowledge.[2] He tallies every fleck and speckle, every deed great or small—however concealed. He deigns to accept the good works of worshippers, however scant, extending forgiveness for their sins, however numerous.

Yet, He shall take them to account, that every soul may learn what it has fetched, and see what she offered and withheld—that the soul may know that without vigilance and self-examination in this world it is but wretched and ruined on the open plain of Resurrection. Even after striving, self-examination and vigilance, if not for God's kindly acceptance of the soul's medley offerings, she would be discomfited and defeated.

Exalted then is He whose grace embraces and comprehends every servant and in whose mercy is immersed—utterly submerged—every created being in this world and the next.

Hearts are distended and opened for faith through the gifts of God's grace. Through the good fortune of His success (*tawfīq*), the limbs are bound to acts of worship and discipline. In the beauty of His guidance (*hidāya*), the darkness of ignorance is dispelled and banished. Through His support (*ta'yīd*) and aid (*nuṣra*) are the devil's ruses foiled.

By the gentleness of His solicitude (*ʿināya*) most good deeds become preponderant upon weighing. And He facilitates what good works are facilitated. From God [every] gift, every reward, every banishing or drawing nigh, every cause for happiness and distress.

Prayers upon Muḥammad, leader of the prophets; and upon his household, the masters of the pure; and upon his Companions, the exemplars of the God-fearing.

Now, God has said, *We shall place scales of justice for the Day of Resurrection, so that not a soul shall be treated unjustly. There is not a mustard seed too small that we shall not bring it forth, for We are the best keepers of accounts.*[3]

*And the Book will be laid down and thou wilt see the evildoers dreading what is in it, saying: 'Woe to us! What a book this is! It leaves out nothing small or great but reckons it.' They shall before them find all they have done. But thy Lord is unjust to no one.*[4]

God said, *on the day when God shall raise them all in order to inform them of their doing. For God reckons* [*what they have done*], *though they will have forgotten it—for God is witness to everything.*[5]

*On that day will people emerge in all their varieties to be shown their deeds. Whoever has done an atom's weight of good shall see it. Whoever has done an atom's weight of evil shall see it.*[6]

*Then will every soul be requited for what it earned, and none shall be treated unjustly.*[7]

*On the day when every soul shall surely find what good it has done and what evil it has done. Its wish will be to be far from the latter. For God cautions ye about Himself.*[8]

*And know that God knows what you harbour inside. Therefore, beware of Him.*[9]

Of all people, those with insight (*arbāb al-abṣār*) will know that God is ever-watchful over them,[A][10] and that they shall be questioned at the Reckoning and that they will be liable for trifling motes of thoughts and glances. They realise that nothing will save them from those perils but perseverance in self-examination and true vigilance and questioning the soul about breaths and movements and examining her thoughts and glances. Whoever examines himself before he is brought to examination, his own account will be lighter at the Resurrection. He shall have his answer when questioned, a good final destiny and return. He who fails to examine himself, his sorrows shall endure. At the courts of Resurrection his haltings shall lengthen—his misdeeds having led him to ignominy and odium.

When this is revealed [to the people of insight], they come to know that nothing but obedience to God will save them from it. God enjoined upon them patience (*ṣabr*) and steadfast commitment[B] (*murābaṭa*). He said,[11] *O ye faithful, have patience, bear up and make a steadfast commitment [to perform the good]*.[12] So, they

[A] As if from a watchtower. This rendering refers us back to the quasi-military concepts of *ribāṭ* and *murābaṭa*, which sometimes included watchtowers and even the minarets of mosques.

[B] I have chosen to translate *murābaṭa*, a difficult term, as 'steadfast commitment'. Ghazālī's choice of words is not coincidental. In the field of ethics, the concept of *murāqaba* (vigilance) is closely associated with *murābaṭa* and *ribāṭ—literally*, 'mounting for battle' (see Introduction). Abū Ḥafṣ ʿUmar al-Suhrawardī (d. 632 /1234) suggested that *ribāṭ*, 'that with which horses are attached', implies that the *murābiṭ* is the frontiersman who seeks to repel what lies 'farther out' (*Kitāb al-ʿawārif*, 104). Figuratively, this would make of *ribāṭ* a struggle against the self (*jihād al-nafs*); the *murābiṭ* would be whoever fights against his own self (*murābiṭ mujāhid nafsihi*) (105). In fact, the 'real' *ribāṭ* consisted of observances of a religio-spiritual, rather than a military, character or some other purely *physical* aspect. According to ʿAbd Allāh b. al-Mubārak, *ribāṭ* is 'the striving against the self and the passions' (*mujāhadat al-nafs wal-hawā*), referring to the 'greater *jihād*', and that this is 'the truth about *jihād*' (*ḥaqq al-jihād* ) (105). This view is commonly understood to be based on the Prophet's saying, 'We returned from the lesser *jihād* to the greater *jihād*' (*ibid.*).

committed themselves, first, by agreeing upon the conditions (*mushāraṭa*),[A] then with vigilance (*murāqaba*), self-examination (*muḥāsaba*), punishment (*muʿāqaba*), renewed striving[B] (*mujāhada*) and, [finally,] censure (*muʿātaba*).[C]

Thus, in steadfast commitment (*murābaṭa*) they have six stations. The explanation of these, the exposition of their essences and merits, the elaboration of the deeds they imply and the root (*aṣl*) of this self-examination are all necessary.

Now, before every accounting (*ḥisāb*)[D] there is the setting of conditions (*mushāraṭa*) and vigilance (*murāqaba*). Upon forfeiture, this is followed by censure (*muʿātaba*) and punishment (*muʿāqaba*).

Let us then explain these stations—and through God is our success.

[A] *Mushāraṭa* (derived from *sharṭ*) should be taken here in the sense of laying down mutually agreed conditions. In fact, laying down the conditions in the morning marks the first part of each day (see next chapter and also Abū Ṭālib al-Makkī, *Qūt*, 1.23, 114-22). Regarding *mushāraṭa*, Ghazālī elsewhere took to task those who availed themselves of logic in their 'religious' polemics (i.e., for religious motives, or *al-maqāṣid al-dīniyya*), because they were wont 'to draw up a list of unassailable conditions for the demonstration' on the assumption that these conditions will produce the same certainty as in a demonstration (Ghazālī, *Munqidh*, 40-1; Watt, *The Faith and Practice of al-Ghazālī*, 36). Their incapacity to satisfy these conditions on religious questions, he alleged, led to 'extreme laxity' in their proofs—presumably due to the weakness of their premises, the conditions.

[B] *Mujāhada* derives from the same root as *jihād*, *j-h-d*. The choice of translating *mujāhada* as 'renewed striving' is due to its position (fifth) within the six stations of *murābaṭa*. It is a 'renewed striving' of the soul after its punishment (*muʿāqaba*; fourth station) for failure to abide by the conditions of the first station (*mushāraṭa*).

[C] These definitions, or stations, of 'steadfast commitment' (*murābaṭa*) make up the chapters of the *Book of Vigilance and Self-examination*.

[D] *Ḥisāb* and *muḥāsaba* have *ḥ-s-b* for a root. Whereas *muḥāsaba* refers to self-examination, *ḥisāb* means adding or taking account and may refer also to the final Reckoning.

## CHAPTER ONE

# The First Station of Steadfast Commitment: Agreeing Upon the Conditions

KNOW THAT WHEN those who engage in commerce and deal in commodities settle accounts, they seek a healthy profit. Hence, the trader avails himself of his associate, handing him money for the trade and then settling his account with him. It is the same with the intellect (*ʿaql*) as it does commerce on the way to the Hereafter. Its object and profit is the purification of the soul, because its felicity is through this.

Said God Exalted, *He is truly felicitous who purifies* [*his soul*] *and he fails who corrupts it.*[1] The soul's felicity is through good works. The intellect avails itself of the soul in this trade because it uses the soul and subjugates it to what will purify it, just as the trader avails himself of his associate and servant, who trades with [the trader's] money.

Now, as the other party can be adversarial, disputing and rivalling him for profit, first, he needs to agree on the conditions; second, to be vigilant with him; third, to call him to account; and fourth, to punish or censure him.[2] By the same token, the intellect first needs to set the conditions for the soul (*mushāraṭat al-nafs*); then to assign tasks to it, lay down the conditions, guide it to the paths of felicity and force it to undertake such paths without for a single moment neglecting to keep vigilant over it. Whenever, on the other hand, the intellect neglects the soul it will find nothing but disloyalty in it and the loss of capital—just like the disloyal servant who, left at liberty, may abscond with the money.

When all is spoken for, [the intellect] has to call the soul to account and demand that it fulfil what conditions he has imposed upon it. For the gain of this commerce is the highest paradise (*al-firdaws al-aʿlā*), the arrival at the Lote Tree (*sidrat al-muntahā*)[A] with the prophets and those who bear witness. Meticulous self-accounting is far more important in this [respect] than [meticulousness] in worldly gains, insignificant as these are in comparison with the [ultimate] end of felicity. For whatever they may be, they are destined to end and to cease. There is no good in an ephemeral good. On the contrary, an ephemeral evil is better than an ephemeral good, because once the ephemeral evil ceases an enduring joy comes with the interruption—the evil having ended. Whereas the ephemeral good, once interrupted, becomes continual regret once the good ends.

This is why it is said,
The greatest distress for me is in joy,
Certain it will turn is he who possesses it

It behoves every resolute person with faith in God and the Last Day not to omit calling his soul to account—to restrict its movements and repose, thoughts and steps. For, every breath of life is a precious gem that has no substitute. One may purchase with it a treasure the felicity of which is everlasting.[3] The expiry of these breaths, when they are forfeited or wasted on what only procures ruin, is a great and stupendous loss which no reasonable soul can permit.

Thus rising in the morning, his morning duties discharged,[B] the servant of God ought to devote his heart for a while to set-

[A] *Sidrat al-muntahā*, beyond which none may pass, is an expression found in the Qurʾān (Q. xxxiv.16 and liii.14-16), where the Lote Tree marks the farthest point of spiritual accomplishment. A thorny, fruit-bearing shrub in the wild, it is thornless when cultivated. This rather paradoxical character has made it a power symbol.

[B] Morning ablution and prayers.

ting the conditions (*mushāraṭa*) for his soul. Just as the trader, upon handing over the goods to the person with whom he trades, reserves the meeting to laying down the conditions for him. [The servant of God] should say to his soul, 'The only commodity I have is my life. As it dissipates so does the capital, and therewith the hope of trade and the search for gain. On this new day God has granted me respite and delayed my appointed time. He has graced me this. Should He take me back to Him, I would wish that He return me to the world for just a day to rectify my error in that. [O my soul,] know you will die and will be brought back [to your Lord].[4] And so beware, O beware of losing this day, as each breath is but a priceless jewel. O my soul, know that a day and night are twenty-four hours.'

As one report says: For every day and night, the servant of God will be shown twenty-four vaults, the one ranged after the other.[A] When one vault opens for him,[5] he finds it filled with the light of the good works he performed during that hour. He is granted joy and happiness and delight at witnessing these lights—his access to the Almighty King. Were this joy to be dispensed to the people of Hell, they would no longer feel the pain of the fire. Another dark, sombre vault opens up for the servant, diffusing its stench and shrouding him with its darkness, this being the hour when he disobeyed God. His only award will be terror and alarm. Should the people of Paradise be allotted these, their paradisal pleasures would surely be spoiled. Then another, empty vault opens[6] for the servant of God, [this time] bringing him nothing that either pleases or displeases him.[7] This is the hour when he slept or was absent-minded or preoccupied with something of this world which is merely permissible. Its emptiness distresses him.[8] Here, he feels cheated in the same way that a person capable of great gains and possessions feels when he is so neglectful and careless that he forfeits them. Suffice it to mention only the distress and the disillusion. This is how the

[A] ʿIraqi 7.

vaults of every moment of his lifetime will be exposed to him.[9]

[The servant of God] will then tell his soul, 'Endeavour today to replenish your vaults, and do not let them be empty of the treasures which occasion your wealth. Do not incline towards idleness, meekness or slackness. Else, you will miss what others may perceive of the loftiest heights,[10] and all you shall have is distress, from which you will not separate even if you enter Paradise. For the pain of the disillusion and the distress is unbearable even without the torment of the fire.'

Someone once said, 'Suppose the offender is forgiven. Will he not have missed out on the reward of the righteous?' He was alluding to the disillusion and the distress. Said God, *The day that assembles you for the Day of the Assembly—that is the day of mutual disillusion.*[11]

That, then, is [the servant of God's] counsel to his soul about the moments [of his life]; after which he proffers counsel about his seven members—the eye, ear, tongue, stomach, pudenda, hands and foot—handing them over to her. For these are the subjects at the service of the soul in this commerce. Through them its commercial dealings are carried out. Verily, hell has seven doors each [leading] to a separate division. These doors are designated to him who disobeys God through these members—and so [he] counsels [the soul] to guard against their disobedience.

*The eye.* One ought to guard it from looking at the face of someone who is not a close relation (*maḥram*)[A] or towards the faultiness (*ʿawra*)[B] of a Muslim, or looking condescendingly at a Muslim—in short, against every unwarranted inquisitiveness. For God shall question His servant as much about excessive gawking as for excessive speech.

When the servant turns his eye away from such, it will only

[A] That is, looking at women who are not related to him and whom he can legally marry.

[B] We have translated *ʿawra* here as 'faultiness' but it includes all that one wishes not to be known or seen, including one's exposed body.

be satisfied[12] if he preoccupies it with whatever pertains to its own commerce and gain. [The eye] was created to gaze at the wonders of God's design with consideration; to gaze at the good works for [the purpose of] emulation; to gaze at the Book of God and the way of His Messenger and to study the books of wisdom from which to take admonition and benefit.

This is how the case of each and every [bodily] member, especially the tongue and stomach [below], ought to be elaborated.

*The tongue*. [We include] the tongue because it is loose by nature and has no trouble moving—great is its surreptitious felony! Among the issues we mentioned in the *Book of the Defects of the Tongue*[A] were mendacity, calumny, exculpation of oneself, disapproval of people and foods, cursing, execration of foes, and prolixity, etc. [The tongue] has to do with all of this. And yet, it is created for invoking [God], remembrance, reiterating knowledge, teaching, guiding the servants of God to His path, reconciling people and other benefits. [The servant of God] must make it conditional upon the soul that it move the tongue during the day only in invocation [of God]. Thus, the utterance of the believer becomes an invocation, his gaze an admonition [for him], his silence a contemplation. *And not a word does he utter than a watchful sentinel shall [stand] by him at the ready.*[13]

*The stomach*. [The servant of God] imposes on it the abandonment of gluttony, the reduction in the eating of licit [food] and the avoidance of what is doubtful. He forbids it appetites, sets forth the limit according to necessity, lays down the condition that if the soul negates any of this it shall, in punishment, be denied the indulgences of the stomach, and therefore it will miss out on more than it gained through its appetites.

In like manner, [the servant of God] sets down the conditions for the soul[14] with respect to all the members. To investigate all this would be lengthy, for the transgressions and acts of piety[15] of the bodily members are already clear.

[A] Book XXIV of the *Revival of the Religious Sciences*.

[The servant of God] then resumes counselling [the soul] on the regular pious duties he repeats day and night, which are then followed by the supererogatory tasks he is capable of and can multiply. He arranges their particularities and modes, and how to prepare for each.

These are conditions he needs every day. Yet, if man accustoms his soul[16] to their imposition for a few days and his soul consents to make good on all, he can dispense with the setting of conditions (*mushāraṭa*). If he is obeyed in some, then the need to repeat the conditions for the rest remains; although every day brings forth a new concern, [some] current event calling for a new verdict, and God has a right over him in all. This is all the more [true] of those who are preoccupied with a worldly act due to governing, trading or teaching. For seldom comes a day without a new event [requiring] him to apply God's right upon it. Therefore, it is incumbent upon the servant to impose uprightness on his soul [in these matters] and the obligation to truth in its progress and to caution it about the outcome of neglect. He [must] admonish it as one admonishes the insubordinate runaway servant. For the soul is by nature refractory to pious acts, rebellious against servanthood. Nevertheless, admonitions and discipline have their effect on it—*and remind [people], for remembrance avails the faithful.*[17]

This—and what is similar to it—is the first station of steadfast commitment in relation to the soul. It is self-examination before the act;[18] self-examination is sometimes after the act, sometimes before it for the purpose of cautioning. Said God, *Know that God knows what is in your souls and take warning from Him.*[19] That is for the future.

Every consideration of quantity and measure aims to know what is more and what is less, and is called self-examination. God's servant reflects on what he encounters in the course of his day in order to tell his additions from his omissions through self-examination.

Said God, *O ye faithful, when ye taketh the path of God be exacting;*[20] *O ye faithful, if an immoral person comes to you with an announcement, be exacting;*[21] *We have created man, and We know how his soul prompts him.*[22] God mentioned this to caution and counsel prudence in the future.

ʿIbāda b. al-Ṣāmit related that the Prophet (may God bless him and grant him peace) had admonished someone who had asked him for advice, 'When you encounter something, ponder its consequences. If it is well-advised, endorse it. If it is offensive, desist from it.'[23]

A learned man said, 'If you want the intellect to prevail over passion, then do not act upon the appetite until you look into the consequence. For regrets dwell longer in the heart than the levity of appetite.'

Said Luqmān, 'Seeing the consequence preserves the faithful from regret.'

Shaddād b. Aws related that the Prophet (may God bless him and grant him peace) said, 'He is astute who subjugates his soul and acts for what lies beyond death. He is foolish who lets his soul follow its appetites and then wishes for God'[24]—where 'subjugates his soul' means 'calls it to account.' The Day of Religion[A] is the day of reckoning. [In the Qur'ān] it is asked, *Have we a debt owed?*—in other words, are we called to account?

Said ʿUmar [b. al-Khaṭṭāb], 'Call yourselves to account before being called to account. Weigh yourselves before being weighed. Make ready for the greatest [Day of] Judgement.'[25] He wrote to Abū Mūsā al-Ashʿarī, 'Call yourself to account in comfort [while you can] before the accounting is severe.'[26]

He asked Kaʿb [al-Aḥbār],[B] 'How do you view [the matter of the soul] in God's Book?'[27] And he added, 'Woe unto the earthly creditor from the Heavenly Creditor!' raising the scourge at him, 'Save he who calls his own soul to account.'

[A] Ghazālī uses the common etymological root of the verb *dāna* ('to subjugate' or 'to put in debt') and the noun *dīn* ('religion') to connect *dāna nafsahu* ('to subjugate his soul' or 'to put his soul in debt') to *yawm al-dīn* ('Day of Religion' or 'Day of Reckoning').

[B] A Yemenite Jewish scholar, at the time, who converted to Islam.

Replied Kaᶜb, 'O Commander of the Faithful, [your word] is identical to what is in the Torah. There is not a letter different between the two;[28] [the Torah says:] he who calls his own soul to account.'

All this indicates accounting for the future, for [the Prophet] said, '[He] who subjugates his soul acts for what lies beyond death…,'[29] which implies first of all weighing matters, then assessing them, studying, planning, then embarking upon and implementing them.

CHAPTER TWO

# The Second Steadfast Commitment: Vigilance

IF MAN PRESCRIBES and makes conditional upon his soul what has been mentioned above, then nothing remains but to be vigilant with it when it rushes to actions and to scrutinise it with a watchful eye. For [the soul] abandoned commits transgression and corruption.

Let us discuss the merit of vigilance and then its degrees.

## *The Merit of Vigilance*

Regarding the merit [of vigilance], Gabriel was asked about the doing of good (*iḥsān*).[A] He replied, 'Worshipping God as if you were looking at Him.' The Prophet said, 'Worship God as if you were looking at Him. Though you see Him not, He sees you.'[1]

Said God, *Is He not then the One who watches over everything which the soul earns?*[2] *Knoweth he not that God doth see?*[3] *For God examines thee;*[4] *And those who respect their trusts and covenants and those who uphold their testimonies.*[5]

Ibn al-Mubārak once said to a man, 'Watch ye God (Exalted is He)!' The man asked him to explain his view. 'Act always as if you saw God Almighty and Majestic,' replied Ibn al-Mubārak.

Said ʿAbd al-Wāḥid b. Zayd, 'When my master watches me, I take notice of nothing else.'[6]

[A] *Iḥsān* implies improvement, perfection and other allied meanings, not just a blanket 'doing the good'. This is especially true in Sufism.

Abū ʿUthmān al-Maghribī said that the best thing which man demands of himself is self-examination and vigilance, and to manage his actions through knowledge.[7]

Said Ibn ʿAṭāʾ, 'The best act of piety is continual vigilance at every moment over the truth.'[8]

Said Jurayrī, 'Our affairs are built on two principles: that you keep your soul vigilant for the sake of God and that you manifestly uphold knowledge.'[9]

Said Abū ʿUthmān [al-Nīsābūrī] that Abū Ḥafṣ [ʿAmr b. Maslama] told him, 'When you sit with people, admonish yourself and your heart. Be not beguiled by their gathering, for they examine only your exterior while God examines your interior.'[10]

It is told that a learned master of this community had a young pupil whom he used to honour and promote. A friend of his then asked him, 'How could you honour someone so young when we are [his] elders?' So, he asked for several birds. He gave each of [his friends] a bird and a knife, saying, 'Let each of you slaughter his bird at a place none can see you.' He handed the same to the youth, telling him what he had told the others.

Everyone returned with his slaughtered bird, but the youth returned with the live bird in hand. He was asked, 'Why have you not slaughtered as your friends have slaughtered?'

'I found no place where no one could see me,' he said, 'for God saw me everywhere.' They commended him for being so watchful, saying, 'Right you are, may you be honoured.'[11]

It is told that when Zulaykhā was alone with Yūsuf, she stood up and covered the face of an idol of hers.[12] Yūsuf asked her, 'What is the matter? Are you shamed by the leer of the inanimate (*murāqabat al-aṣnām*) and I should not be by the watchful gaze of the almighty King?'[13]

One tradition tells of a young lad who had been seducing a servant-girl. She told him, 'Are you not ashamed?'

He replied, 'Ashamed from whom? Who can see us but the stars?'

'But what of their Maker?' she said.[14]

A man asked Junayd, 'What can help me avert my gaze (*ghaḍ al-basar*)?'[A]

'With your knowledge that the sight of the One who sees you precedes your view of whatever you see.'[15]

Said Junayd, 'He will verily obtain confirmation through vigilance who fears losing his share from his Lord Almighty and Majestic.'[16]

Said Mālik b. Dīnār,[17] 'The Gardens of Eden are among the Gardens of Firdaws. In them are *ḥūr* created from the flowers of Paradise.'

He was asked, 'And who inhabits it?'

'God Almighty and Majestic says, "Those who inhabit the Gardens of Eden are those who, about to sin, remember my majesty and, thus, heed Me. They bend over backwards from fear of Me, My might and majesty. For I care about the suffering of the earth's inhabitants. When I see those who hunger and thirst for fear of Me, I avert the punishment (*ʿadhāb*) from them."'[18]

When Muḥāsibī was asked about vigilance, he said, 'It begins with the heart's knowledge of the proximity of the Lord.'[19]

Said Murtaʿish, 'Vigilance is attending to one's secret [interior] in order to be[20] wary of what lies hidden at every moment and with every utterance.'[21]

It is told that God said to His angels, 'You have been charged with the exterior, while I watch over the interior.'[22]

Said Muḥammad b. ʿAlī al-Tirmidhī, 'Examine yourself before the One who ever sees you. Offer gratitude to the One whose blessings to you never cease. Be obedient to the One you cannot but need. Show humility to the One whose dominion and power you cannot escape.'[23]

Said Sahl [al-Tustarī], 'The heart is adorned with nothing better or nobler than the servant's knowledge that God sees him as he is.'[24]

[A] A Qur'ānic expression having to do with modest behaviour (see verses XXIV.30-1, XLIX.3 and XXXI.19).

Someone said that these words of God, *God well pleased with them and they with Him—all this for such as fear his Lord,*[25] referred to one who heeds his Lord, examines and equips himself for the Hereafter.

Dhū al-Nūn was asked, 'How does the servant attain to Paradise?' He answered, 'With five [traits]: uprightness (*istiqāma*) with no prevarication, striving (*ijtihād*) without distraction, being vigilant of God Exalted both secretly and openly, expectation of death and readiness for it, self-examination before being taken to account.'

It is said:

> If you are free for a day in time say not: I am free,
> but say: I have someone watching over me.
> Think neither that God hath forgotten an hour
> nor that what ye concealeth from Him is absent.Do
> you not see that the day is faster in coming,
> that tomorrow it is near to those that await it.

Said Ḥumayd al-Ṭawīl to Sulaymān b. ʿAlī al-ʿUẓnī, 'Teach me.' He said, 'If you disobey God in isolation without knowing that God sees you, then you have committed a grave sin. But if you surmise that He sees you not, then you have rejected Him (*kafarta*).'

Said Sufyān al-Thawrī, 'You must be vigilant of the One from whom nothing is hidden. You must be expectant of the One who fulfils. You must beware of the One who can punish.'

Said Farqad al-Sabakhī,[26] 'The hypocrite looks on. When he sees no one, he embarks upon evil—for he watches people, not God Exalted.'

Said ʿAbd Allāh b. Dīnār, 'I left for Mecca with ʿUmar b. al-Khaṭṭāb and, on the way, we stopped for a rest. A shepherd came down to us from the mountain. He [ʿUmar] said to him, "O shepherd, sell me a sheep from your herd."

'The shepherd replied, "I belong to someone."

'"Say to your master that it was devoured by a wolf."

'"Where is God then?"

"ʿUmar wept. Returning in the morning, he bought the shepherd from his master and freed him, saying, "With this word you are freed in this world. I hope it frees you in the Hereafter.""[27]

## An Exposition of the Reality and Degrees of Vigilance

Know that the reality of vigilance is to be aware of the one watching (*raqīb*) and to turn attention to him. Therefore, one who is cautious about a matter because of someone else is said to be vigilant of someone and watchful of his own flank. In other words, vigilance is a state of the heart that results from a kind of knowledge. This state causes the action in the heart and the limbs.

The 'state' is the heart's heedfulness of the one who watches and preoccupation with him; the heart turns to him, observes him and applies itself to him. As to the 'knowledge which gives rise to this state',[28] this is the knowledge that God sees the hearts, knows everyone's innermost secrets, watches the deeds of the servants and oversees in every soul what it has earned. For Him, the secret of the heart is exposed, much like the exposed face for people—nay, more so.

When this knowledge becomes certain—I mean devoid of doubt—it overcomes and dominates the heart. Not all indubitable knowledge[29] prevails over the heart—such as the knowledge of death. When [certain knowledge] subdues the heart, it makes it mindful in deference to the one who watches and it turns its attention to him.

Those who are certain in this knowledge are those who are near to God (*muqarrabūn*). They comprise the perfectly truthful (*ṣiddīqūn*) and the people of the right hand (*aṣḥāb al-yamīn*). Therefore, their vigilance is on two levels.

*First level.* The first level is the vigilance of the perfectly truthful among those near to God. This is the vigilance of glorification and exaltation. It is when the heart is engrossed in the awareness of this exaltation, crushed by awe; therefore, it has no room truly to consider another. We will not detain ourselves by describing the deeds of this vigilance, which is confined to the heart.

The members, for their part, are incapable of turning towards the lawful and away from the prohibited [on their own]. When they move [during the performance of] pious deeds, they are like everything used for that purpose. They do not direct or confirm [themselves] in their set course. Rather, the flock is fully set [on its path] by the dominion of the shepherd. The heart is the shepherd. When [the heart] becomes absorbed in the One worshipped, the members [in turn] are employed without hindrance according to a fixed and straight course.

This is the person with a single focus, for God has spared him other foci.[A] Someone who attains to this level so disregards creation that he neither sees another's presence, even with his eyes wide open, nor hears what he is told, even though he is not deaf to it. For example, he may pass by his son without speaking to him; and as when a person says to his detractor, 'When you [next] encounter me, stir me.'[B]

Do not think this farfetched. You will find its analogy in those hearts that exalt earthly kings, that are subservient to the kings and hardly sensing what overtakes them in the presence of kings because they are so absorbed by them. For the heart can become preoccupied with a trivial thing of the world, and the man—while walking—can become immersed in thinking about it and may walk on past the place he was headed for and forget the concern that motivated him [in the first place].

[A] A paraphrase of: 'God has spared him his world' (Ibn Māja, *Zuhd*, II.1375, no. 4106; *Muqaddima*, I.94, no. 257). *Hamm* is an important concept, especially in *taṣawwuf*. Ghazālī implies that the unitary focus on God should govern one's actions in this world precisely to avoid being governed by the myriad cares of the world, which designates what is other than God.

[B] This is a question of focus. Ghazālī is not saying that one should go through life oblivious to people and surroundings, but on the contrary to ignore any distractions that draw attention away from whatever one consciously does for the sake of God. See the text below relating to the second level 'before acting'.

ʿAbd al-Wāḥid b. Zayd was asked,[30] 'In this age, do you know of a man who, self-absorbed, is oblivious of people?'

'I only know of one man who will momentarily come to you.' And just as quickly entered ʿUtba [b. Abān b.] al-Ghulām.[31] ʿAbd al-Wāḥid asked him, 'Where have you come from, O ʿUtba?' He replied from such-and-such a place. He was on his way to the market.

'Whom did you meet on the way?'

'I saw no one.'[32]

It is related that Yaḥyā b. Zakariyyā[A] (peace be upon them both) once met a woman. He pushed her and she fell over. Asked why he acted thus, he said, 'I thought she was only a wall.'[33]

It is narrated someone once said[34] that he encountered a group of people shooting [arrows]. One person sat far from them. I approached him, wanting to speak with him. But he said, 'The remembrance of God is more desirable.'

'You are alone,' I said.

'My Lord and my two angels are with me,' he said.

'Which of these [people present] will win out?' I asked.

'The one whom God forgives.'

'Where is the path,' I asked. He pointed towards heaven, rose and walked away, saying, 'Most of Your creatures are distracted from You.'[35]

These are the words of someone absorbed in the vision of God, speaking only from God and hearing only through Him. Such a person need not watch his tongue and limbs, for they move only through what he is in.

[Abū Bakr] Shiblī entered upon Abū al-Ḥusayn al-Nūrī, who was in retreat. He found him tranquil and good company. Nothing about him seemed to move. He asked him, 'How did you acquire such vigilance and repose?'

'From a cat we used to own. Whenever it wanted to hunt, it stood poised upon a rock without a hair moving.'

[A] The Arabic equivalent of 'John the Baptist'.

Said Abū ʿAbd Allāh b. Khafīf, 'I departed from Egypt towards Ramalah[A] in order to meet Abū ʿAlī al-Rūdhbārī. ʿĪsā b. Yūnus al-Miṣrī, known as the Ascetic, told me that in Tyre[B] a youth and an adult shared the same state of vigilance. "If you but looked at them, you would benefit from them."

'I arrived in Tyre famished and thirsty, with only a rag around my waist and nothing on my shoulders. I entered the mosque and there sat two men facing the *qibla*.[C] I greeted them, but they did not answer. I greeted them a second and third time.[36] Still I heard no response.

'"I implore you, by God, to return my salutation," I said. Then the youth raised his head from beneath his patched gown (*marqaʿatihi*)[37] and looked at me, saying, "O Ibn Khafīf, the world is paltry and nothing but the paltry remains of the paltry. So, take the great from the paltry. Ibn Khafīf, the smaller your preoccupation, the freer you are for our meeting [with God]." He captivated me.

'Then he tilted his head in [another] direction. I remained with them for the noon and afternoon prayers, as my hunger, thirst and pains had gone away. In the afternoon I said, "Admonish me!" The youth raised his head to me and said, "O Ibn Khafīf, we are companions in misfortune, we have no words of admonition." I stayed with them for three days, neither eating nor drinking nor sleeping. I saw neither food nor drink with them.

'On the third day, I said to myself that I shall entreat them to preach to me that I may benefit from their admonition. Then the youth raised his head and told me, "O Ibn Khafīf, you must befriend the one who reminds you of God when you see him. May his dread befall your heart and may he admonish you in the language of his deed, not that of his words. And so farewell, leave us."'

[A] A city in Palestine.
[B] A seaport in Lebanon.
[C] Direction of Mecca for ritual purposes.

This then is the level of the vigilant whose hearts are dominated by exaltation and glorification. They have no capacity for anything else.

*Second level.* The second level is the vigilance of the pious (*wariʿūn*) among the people of the right hand. This group is that of those whose hearts are overcome by the certainty that God sees the hearts' interiors and exteriors. However,[38] the awareness of divine majesty does not dazzle them. On the contrary, their hearts keep within the limit of balance and are capable of attending to states and deeds. While performing deeds, however, they never fail to be vigilant. They are certainly dominated by shame (*ḥayā'*) before God, advancing and retreating only upon confirmation in it. They abstain from what might disgrace them on [the Day of] Resurrection. But since they [already] consider that God sees them in the world, they have no need to await the Resurrection.

You will recognise the difference between the two levels from the gazes [of onlookers] (*mushāhadāt*). You may be performing certain acts by yourself, but then a youth or a woman comes over who, you learn, has seen you and you are embarrassed. You sit in a more becoming manner, alert not to reverence and exaltation but to shame. Although it neither amazed nor engrossed you, [the boy's or woman's] sight did arouse shame in you. Then some king or eminent person walks in. You take to exaltation, abandoning everything else[39] that occupied you; without embarrassment because of him. This is how the levels of worshippers differ in the vigilance of God Exalted.

He who is at this [second] level needs to be vigilant about everything he does and does not do, his thoughts and glances—in short, his every choice. He is responsible for them in two respects: before the act and during the act. Before the act, he should observe what appears to him and what actually gives rise to his thought. Is it for God, in particular? Or does the passion of the soul or adherence to the devil give rise to it? This should cause him to pause and settle it, until it is revealed to him through the light of God.

If it is for God, he may complete it. If it is for something other than God, he feels shame before Him and desists, his soul pained by his wish, attention and inclination. He recognises the evil of his soul's commission, the scandal of its pursuit, and that it is its own foe unless God restores it through His protection.

Above all, this pause is a duty which must be imposed and which no one can escape.[40] As the report says, 'The servant [of God] knows that his every activity, however small, contains three accountings (*dawāwīn*). The first is 'why'; the second 'how' and the third 'for whom'.'[41] The 'why' implies 'why have you done this'? Were you obliged to do it for your Master or have your desire and passion caused you to be so inclined?

If the person is released from this, being obliged to act thus because of his Master, he is asked the second accountings: 'How did you do this?' For every deed has a condition and a judgement by God; its measure, time and quality are discernible only through knowledge. Therefore, the person is asked: 'How did you act—with verified[42] knowledge or through ignorance and supposition?'

If he is released from this, the third accountings is brought forward—the questioning about sincerity. He will be asked: 'For whom have you acted? Was it purely for God's countenance to fulfil your utterance of "There is no deity but God", for which God must reward you? Or to dissimulate a mortal like yourself, [in which case] take your recompense from him. Or for immediate, mundane reasons; in which case your claim will be redeemed in this world alone. Or inadvertently, in which case you will not be rewarded, and your deed and effort will have been futile.' 'If it was done for anyone but Me, then you shall earn loathing and wrath, for you are My servant. You eat what I provide, luxuriate in what comfort I give and then you act for another's sake. Yet, you heard Me say, *Verily, those whom ye call upon besides God as servants are servants like you*;[43] *The things ye worship besides God have no provisions to give thee; seek then sustenance from God, worship Him and be grateful to Him.*[44] Woe to you! Have you not heard Me say, *Is it to God that sincere devotion is done?*'[45]

When the servant of God knows that he is faced with these

demands and reproaches, he will call his soul to account before it is called to account. And he will prepare an answer to the question, and ensure that the answer is correct.[46] He will [no longer] advance or retreat without verification; he will not move an eyelid or a fingertip without forethought.

Said the Prophet to Muʿādh [b. Jabal], '[Each] man will be asked about the kohl around his eyes, and the tads[47] of earth on his two fingers and his touching of his brother's garb.'[48]

Said Ḥasan [al-Baṣrī], 'When one of them wanted to give alms he reflected and gave careful consideration. If it was for God, he performed it.'[49] He said, 'God is merciful towards a servant who, arrested by a concern of his, pursues it if it is for God, but holds back when it is for something else.'[50]

In a tradition, Saʿd [b. Abī Waqqāṣ] said that Salmān [al-Fārisī] had advised him, 'Fear God, in [all] your concerns, if you have any.'

Said Muḥammad b. ʿAlī,[A] 'He is faithful who is an unhurried overseer facing his care—he is not like a wood gatherer at night.'[B]

This, then, is the first consideration of vigilance. Nothing rescues from this but firm knowledge and a true understanding of the secrets of actions, the depths of the soul and the subterfuges of the devil. He who knows not himself, his Lord or his foe, Iblīs, and neither knows what accords with his passion nor distinguishes it from what God loves,[51] but accepts it in his intention, care, thought, rest and activity—will not find protection in this [kind of] vigilance. Indeed, most people will exhibit ignorance in what God dislikes, *believing they are fashioning improvements*.[52]

Do not think that the person ignorant of what is capable of being learned may be excused. Far from it! Seeking knowledge is obligatory for all Muslims. This is why two prayer cycles (*rakʿa*) by a knowledgeable person are better than a thousand by an ignorant

[A] Son of Ḥusayn b. ʿAlī b. Abī Ṭālib.

[B] That is, acts randomly without seeing.

one. This is because the former knows about the evils of the soul, the subterfuges of the devil and loci of illusion—consequently, he guards against them. The ignoramus, on the other hand, does not know all of this, so how could he be wary of it? He is always in hardship. The devil is pleased with him and takes malicious joy. We seek God's protection from the ignoramus and from ignorance and negligence, for this is the root of distress, the basis of loss.

God has ruled that every servant must be vigilant with his soul when contemplating an act and undertaking to use one of his members. Let him pause at the contemplation and at the undertaking until the light of knowledge reveals to him either that the act would be for God and that he should complete it; or that it would be due to the soul's passion and that he should guard against it, and keep the heart from pondering and concentrating on it.

If the first false notion is not repelled, it may give rise to a desire and the desire to a contemplation, the contemplation to a firm resolve, the resolve to a deed and the deed to ruin and odium. One ought to cut the substance of evil at its source of origin, namely, the notion (*khāṭir*), for everything follows behind it.

Whenever the matter seems obscure for God's servant or the situation appears murky and inexplicable, let him ponder it in the light of knowledge. Let him seek refuge in God from the subterfuge the devil spins by means of the [servant's] passion. But if he is able neither of striving nor meditating on his own, let him find enlightenment through religious scholars, but let him take flight from the misguided scholars devoted to this world—flight from the devil. More emphatically, God revealed to David (peace be upon him), 'Ask no scholar about Me who is inebriated with love of this world. He will sever you from My affection. These are the ones who cut off the path for My servants.' Therefore, the hearts that are obscured by the love of this world, that frenzy over it and greatly covet it are veiled from the light of God. The illumination of the lights of the hearts is the presence of lordship. How then can anyone be illuminated by them who turns his back on them, accepts their enemy, hates them passionately and finds them repugnant? Those are but the desires of this world.

Let the seeker (*murīd*) focus primarily on the judgements of knowledge or on his search for a scholar who is averse to this world or whose desire for it is weak—if not for one who harbours no desire for it at all. God's Messenger (may God bless him and grant him peace) said, 'God loves the critical gaze upon doubtful matters and the accomplished intellect at the onslaught of desires'[53]—combining two things, which in [their] reality are inseparable. He whose intellect cannot restrain the desires does not possess the [requisite] critical view of doubtful matters. This is why God's Messenger stated, 'He that yields to a sin: his intellect shall depart from him never to return to him again.'[54] For, no matter what the weak intellect with which the human being is fortuned determines, he will embark on its obliteration and annihilation through the temptation of sin.

In these times, knowledge about the evils of deeds has been extinguished. People have abandoned these sciences;[55] they busy themselves with mediating differences among the population that are stirred up by the adherence to desires, claiming this is the true jurisprudence (*fiqh*). They separate that science—namely, the jurisprudence of religion (*fiqh al-dīn*)—from other sciences and devote themselves solely to the jurisprudence of the world (*fiqh al-dunyā*), which is intended only to ward off the worries of the hearts and to pave the way for jurisprudence of religion. Yet, the jurisprudence of the world is part of religion (*dīn*) [only] by way of jurisprudence.[A] According to the report, 'Today you are at a

[A] In other words, jurisprudence of the world serves 'religion', being systematic and practically oriented—in other words, *jurisprudential*. Ghazālī understood religion too as a practical pursuit (see introduction to my translation of the *Book of Intention*). As a systematic pursuit, however, jurisprudence as such assists in the practical application of religion, though it cannot substitute itself for either religion or what he calls here the 'jurisprudence of religion', or literally, the proper 'discernment' or understanding of religious precepts. In this manner, the world and its preoccupations may be deemed necessary for salvation but they do not dictate its terms.

time when the best among you is he who forges ahead (*musāri*). A time will come when the best among you will be the cautious (*mutathabbit*).'

This is why a group of the Prophet's Companions took pause regarding the fight with the Iraqī and Syrian [soldiery allied with Muʿāwiya], as the matter was unclear for them—[among whom were Companions] like Saʿd b. Abī Waqqāṣ, ʿAbd Allāh b. ʿUmar, Usāma and Muḥammad b. Maslama and others.

Someone who does not pause (*tawaqqaf*) when in doubt follows his passions, proud of his opinion. He is like those whom the Messenger of God described when he said, 'If you see submission to avarice, adherence to passion, and admiration of each his own opinion, you must be responsible for your own self.'[56] Anyone who proceeds with a doubtful matter without verification contradicts what God said, *Pursue not that which thou knowest not*.[57] The Prophet said, 'Beware of conjecture, for conjecture is the most deceptive thing uttered.'[58] He meant by this conjecturing without any evidence—for example, any from the common run who consults his heart over an unclear matter and follows his conjectures.

It was against the difficulty and magnitude of this that [Abū Bakr] al-Ṣiddīq had prayed, 'O God, show me the real truth and endow me with adherence to it; show me what is truly false and endow me with its avoidance. Make it not so obscure for me that I follow passion.'

Said Jesus (peace be upon him), 'There are three [kinds] of things: one the rectitude of which is clear, so adhere to it; another the error of which is clear, so avoid it; and [a third] which is obscure to you, so leave it to he who understands it.'

One of the Prophet's prayers was, 'O God, I seek refuge in Thee against making utterance in religion without knowledge.'[59]

For the greatest of God's blessings upon His servants is knowledge and truth unveiled. Faith is a kind of unveiling and knowledge. This is why God graciously said to his servant, *Great is God's favour upon thee*.[60]—by which He meant knowledge. God said, *Ask those who recall [God's message], if ye have not the knowledge;*[61] *Verily, it is for Us to guide;*[62] *Nay, it is for Us to make clear;*[63] *It is for God [to show] the right way.*[64]

Said ʿAlī [Ibn Abī Ṭālib], 'Passion is the accomplice of blindness. Success entails pausing upon hesitation. Yea, nothing banishes care better than certainty and remorse better than effacing the lie. In truthfulness is the salvation. Someone at a distance may be closer than one close by; and it is unusual for one not to have an intimate. The perfectly truthful is he whose inner state (*ghaybuhu*) is truthful. Do not let a suspicion keep you from a beloved. Yea, the best character trait is generosity and from modesty (*ḥayā'*) springs everything comely. Piety (*taqwā*) is the most secure bond. The firmest relation you can assume is between you and God. You have gained from this world what you have tilled for your abode [in the Hereafter].

'Sustenance is [of two kinds]: one which you seek and one that seeks you.[A] If you do not come to it, it will come to you. If you regret what has slipped from you, regret not then what has not occurred. Inquire about what has not happened through what has.

'Things resemble each other. Man rejoices over attaining what would not have missed him and sorrows over losing what he would never have attained.[B] Do not exult over what is given to you in your world. And be not regretful for what you miss of it. Your joy should be in what lies before you, your regret in what is behind you. Your preoccupation should be with your Afterlife, and your care with what lies after death.' Our reason for transmitting these words is ʿAlī's statement 'Success entails pausing upon hesitation.'

[A] Meaning, obtained regardless of effort.

[B] Meaning, that what is destined for him will come to him and what is not he cannot attain; it is not through his own actions that he affects either. Thus, rejoicing and sorrowing are to be viewed from this perspective.

Accordingly, the first consideration[A] for the vigilant person is to look into the matter of concern or the activity: Is it for God or for passion? Said the Prophet (may God bless him and grant him peace), 'A person who perfects his faith has three [traits]: in God he fears no detractor; he boasts about none of his deeds; and faced with two choices—one for the world, the other for the Hereafter—he prefers the Hereafter to the world.'[65] What is disclosed to him about his deeds is, at most, that they are permissible. Unconcerned, he abandons them, because of what the Prophet had said, 'What is comely about a man's Islam is that he forsakes what concerns him not.'

The second consideration is that of vigilance upon the initiation of action—namely, checking how the action [is executed] in compliance with the prerogative of God in the matter, improving the intention in order to complete and perfect the action, and pursuing it as far as possible. These are imperative for him in all his states. For in every state, he is always either active or at rest. If he is wary of God in all of these, he will be well capable of acts of worship before God with intention, good deed and deference to propriety.

When a person is seated, for instance, he ought to sit facing the *qibla*. As the Prophet (may God bless him and grant him peace) said, 'The best sitting is where one faces the *qibla*.'[66] He should not sit cross-legged, as one does not sit like that with kings—for the King of kings sees him.[B]

Said Ibrāhīm b. Adham, 'Once I sat cross-legged when I heard a voice calling out: Is this the way to sit with kings? After that I never again sat down cross-legged.'[67]

When a person sleeps, he ought to sleep on his right-hand side facing the *qibla*. [This and the above are] among the manners

[A] This is a reference to the first of the two considerations mentioned above: vigilance before the act.

[B] The point is not that sitting cross-legged is wrong, but rather sitting inappropriately for the occasion and, more specifically, in a way which is not in keeping with an attitude of vigilance. This is clear from the text below.

(*ādāb*) we have mentioned elsewhere in their proper contexts. All pertain to vigilance. Even relieving oneself has to be according to propriety and should be in keeping with vigilance.

Therefore, the servant of God may act out of obedience, disobedience or permissibility. He is vigilant in acts of obedience through sincerity, completion, deference to propriety and the guarding against evil-doing. Upon acts of disobedience he is vigilant through repentance, remorse, abstention, shame and the use of introspection.[68] With permissible acts he is vigilant through deference to propriety and, finally, by bearing witness to the Benefactor for a blessing and being grateful for it.

In no state is God's servant without a hardship he must forbear, nor a blessing for which he must be grateful. All this is part of vigilance. The servant can never release himself from his duty towards God in any state. This may consist of an act which he has to pursue, something forbidden he must forgo, or an assignment spurring him on quickly towards God's pardon, ahead of God's [other] servants. Or it may be something permissible and salutary for his body and heart, assisting him in his pious deeds. Each one of these has limits, the observance of which perpetuate the vigilance. *And any that transgresses the limits of God wrongs only himself.*[69]

In these three classes [of acts], God's servant must be introspective at every moment. If he is free of obligatory duties (*farā'iḍ*) and capable of supererogatory ones (*faḍā'il*), he must search for the best action and set himself to it. Someone who fails to take the highest profit, when he can, has duped [himself]. Profits are gained by supererogatory acts. Thus the servant takes from his world for his afterlife. As God says, *Nor forget thy portion in this world.*[70]

This can all be secured in a single moment. There are three [kinds of] moments: the moment passed, with no [further] exertion for the servant, whether it ended in toil or comfort; the future moment unreckoned, which the servant does not know whether or not he will live to see and does not perceive what God has decreed for it; finally, the present moment during which he must exert himself and be wary of his Lord.

If the second [kind of] moment does not come to pass for him, he will not grieve its loss. But if it comes to pass, then he may claim his right from it just as he would the first [kind of moment]. He should not carry his hope fifty years forward, for then the resoluteness [required for] vigilance might weary him. Indeed, he should be 'the son of the moment' (*ibn al-waqt*),[A] somewhat like being at his last few breaths. He may well be at his last few breaths without knowing it.

If it is possible that he is at his last breaths, then he must be in a state in which he is not averse to being overtaken by death.[71] All his states must be limited to what Abū Dharr (may God be pleased with him) narrated about the Prophet's utterance, 'The believer journeys for [one of] three things: provisions for the final] destination, improved livelihood or pleasure in something not forbidden.'[72] And in this vein, 'It is incumbent upon the sound of mind to have four moments: a moment where he confides (*yunājī*) in his Lord; a moment to take his soul to account; a moment to ponder what God has made; and a moment devoted to eating and drinking—the latter moment as an aid for the other moments.'[73] The moment when the servant's members are occupied with eating and drinking should not be devoid of a deed which is the best of deeds—namely, remembrance and thought. The food he consumes, for example, contains marvels which, if he contemplates and comprehends them, are superior to most of what the members do.

People differ over this. One group view [food] reflectively (*bi-ʿayn al-tabaṣṣur*):[74] they gaze at the marvels of its [the food's] creation; how animal sustenance is connected with it; how God deemed it a means of subsistence; the creation of the desires[75] that drive towards it; the instruments adapted to making it desirable.

[A] On this concept, cf. T.j. de Boer, "Zamān," *Encyclopaedia of Islam*, First Edition. Retrieved November 10 2014; first appeared online: 2012. [<http://referenceworks.brillonline.com/entries/encyclopaedia-of-islam-1/zama-n-SIM_6070>]

We have explained some of this in the *Book of Thankfulness*.[A] This is the station of the 'people of insight' (*dhawī al-albāb*).

Another group view [food] with loathing and aversion; taking it as a necessity and wishing they were free of it. However, they see that they are subjugated to it and subdued by the desire for it. This is the station of the ascetics (*zāhidūn*).

Yet another group[76] see in the work the Maker, and rise above it towards the attributes of the Creator. This experience brings forth [new] avenues of thinking[77] to be contemplated, avenues which open because of that. This is the highest station, the station of the gnostics (*ʿārifūn*) and the signs of the amorous (*muḥibūn*). For when the one who loves sees his beloved's work, letter and writing, he forgets the work [itself] and his heart becomes engrossed in the maker [of the work].

Everything that recurs to the servant[78] is God's making. When he turns from it to look at the Maker his purview is wide; assuming the doors of the heavenly kingdom (*malakūt*) open for him, and this is very rare indeed.

The fourth group view [food] as desire and longing (*ḥirṣ*). They regret missing out on it and rejoice when they partake of it. They find fault with whatever does not agree with their passion and blame the one who made it, and so they find fault with both the cooking and the cook. They do not know that the agent behind the cooking, the cook and his power and knowledge is God Himself. He who finds fault in God's creation without God's leave blames God. This is why the Prophet (may God bless him and grant him peace) said, 'Do not curse time (*dahr*),[B] for time is God.'[79]

This then is the Second Steadfast Commitment, that of the

[A] Book XXXVI of the *Revival of the Religious Sciences*. See also Eric Ormsby's translation *Al-Ghazālī on Love, Longing, Intimacy and Contentment*, Islamic Texts Society, 2011.

[B] This is not meant in the ordinary sequential or chronological sense of time, but rather in the permanence or simultaneity of time.

continual and uninterrupted vigilance of deeds. It would be too lengthy to expand [further] on it. The above merely shows the way for whoever can master the principles.

## CHAPTER THREE

# The Third Steadfast Commitment: Self-examination After the Act, Recalling the Merit of Examination and Its Reality

WE SHALL DISCUSS the merit of self-examination followed by its reality.

### *The Merit of Self-examination*

Regarding the merit [of self-examination], God says, *O ye faithful, fear God and let the soul look to what [provision] it has sent for the morrow.*[1] This signifies the examination of past acts.

It is why ʿUmar said about this, 'Examine yourselves before you are examined. Weigh before you are weighed.'

According to a tradition, a man came to the Prophet (may God bless him and grant him peace) saying, 'O Messenger of God, give me advice.'

'You seek advice?' replied the Messenger.

'Yea,' the man said.

'When you embark upon something, determine its consequences. If it is right, complete it—if wrong, refrain from it.'[2]

According to a report, the sound of mind must have four moments, one of which is to examine himself.[3]

God says, *Repent to God, ye all, O faithful, that you may attain to happiness.*[4] Repentance is a consideration of the deed after one is freed from it through remorse.

Said the Prophet (may God bless him and grant him peace), 'I seek God's forgiveness and repent to Him a hundred times a day.'[5]

Said God, *When those who fear God are taken by a sudden urge from Satan, they remember [God], and immediately they can see [aright].*[6]

It is said that ʿUmar used to strike his feet at nightfall with a lash of whip, saying, 'What have I done today?'

It is told that Maymūn b. Mahrān said, 'The servant [of God] is not godfearing until he calls himself more strictly to account than he would his associate,' for associates settle their accounts after the act.

It is said that ʿĀ'isha was told by Abū Bakr as he was dying, 'No one is dearer to me than ʿUmar.' Then he said to her, 'What did I say?' She repeated his words. And he said, 'No one is more beloved to me than ʿUmar.' Notice his remark after finishing the [first] utterance: he measured it and substituted another utterance in its place.

In a tradition, Abū Ṭalḥa tells of the time when a bird distracted him from his prayer; weighing this, he offered his walled enclosure as an offering to God in remorse, hoping that this might compensate for what he had missed.[7]

It is reported that [ʿAbd Allāh] Ibn Salām was carrying a bundle of firewood when someone said to him, 'O Abū Yūsuf, any of your children or servants could have spared you this.' He said, 'I wanted to see if my soul would object to it.'

Said al-Ḥasan [al-Baṣrī], 'The faithful one manages his soul and calls it to account for the sake of God. The Reckoning is lighter for a people who examine themselves in this world, but it will be harsher on the Day of Resurrection for those people who deal with this matter without self-examination.' He then explained self-examination, 'The person of faith is confronted by the thing that pleases him and says, "By God, you please me and I am in need of you.[8] But far from it! You are prohibited to me."' This is self-examination before the act. He then said, 'And he forgoes the thing and returns to his soul.' He then said, 'What did I intend by this? "By God, I cannot vouch for it. And, by

God, I shall never repeat this, God willing!"'[A]

Said Anas b. Mālik, 'I was listening to ʿUmar b. al-Khaṭṭāb one day. He went out and I went with him until he passed into an enclosure.[9] I heard him say when he was in the enclosure, and between him and me was the wall, "ʿUmar b. al-Khaṭṭāb, Commander of the Faithful—well done! Verily you will fear God or verily He will punish you!"'[B]

About God's words, *And nay I swear by the self-reproaching soul*,[10] al-Ḥasan [al-Baṣrī] said, 'You will always find the believer reproaching himself: What did I mean by what I said? What was the reason for this food I ate? What was the reason for this drink I drank? The sinful one moves forward without any self-reproach.'[C]

Said Mālik b. Dīnār, 'God was merciful with a servant who said to his soul, "Have you not befriended so-and-so? Have you not befriended?" He then bridled [his soul],[11] placed a halter on it and enjoined upon it the Book of God, which then led him.' This then is self-reproach as will later be discussed.

Said Maymūn b. Mahrān, 'The pious person examines his soul more severely than if he were a tyrannical ruler and a niggardly associate.'

Said Ibrāhīm al-Taymī, 'I imagined myself in paradise eating of its fruits, drinking from its streams and embracing its maidens. Then I imagined myself in the Fire, eating from its infernal tree, drinking its purulence and attending to its chains and shackles. So I said to my soul, "O soul, which do you want?" She said, 'I want to return to the world to do what is right." I said, "You shall have your desire, so go forth."'[12]

[A] Meaning that the person of faith will then say to himself, "By God, I have no excuse for it. And, by God, I shall never repeat this, God willing!"

[B] ʿUmar here is mocking and chastising himself.

[C] It is told that Mujāhid said that the reproaching soul is remorseful about what has come to be and lays blame for it (Zabīdī 113).

Said Mālik b. Dīnār, 'I heard al-Ḥajjāj [b. Yūsuf al-Thaqafī] preaching [from the pulpit], "God is merciful with a man who calls his soul to account before [the account] with another. God is merciful with a man who reins in his deed and considers what he intends by it. God is merciful[13] with a man who considers that by which he will be measured. God is merciful[14] with a man who considers his weight [on the Balance]." [Al-Ḥajjāj] continued to speak thus until he made me weep.'[15]

A companion of al-Aḥnaf b. Qays [al-Tamīmī] said, 'I used to accompany him. His nightly prayer was mostly supplication. He used to approach the lamp and place his finger in it until he felt the flame. Then he would say to himself, "O true believer, what made you do what you did on such-and-such a day? What made you do what you did on such-and-such a day?"'[16]

## *An Exposition of the Reality of Self-examination After the Act*

Know that just as the servant of God has from the beginning of the day to obtain his soul's agreement with truthful admonition, so by day's end he has a time within which to demand an accounting and to examine his soul for all it has or has not done.

In their mundane concerns, the merchants of this world act in similar fashion with their associates at the end of every year, month or day. They are fearful of omitting anything of the world that might be a boon to them. If that were to happen to them, they would have only a few days left [to rectify the balance]. So how can a reasonable man fail to examine his soul about what relates to the danger of eternal damnation or salvation? Surely such indulgence is due to forgetfulness (*ghafla*), failure, and success denied (*qillat al-tawfīq*) [by God]. From this we seek refuge in God.

The examination of an associate implies consideration of the capital, the profit and the loss in order to distinguish the surplus from the loss. If there is a gain in revenue, it is received in full and gratefully. In the event of a loss, it is claimed as a liability and assigned as a future indemnity.

The same holds true for the capital of the worshipper with respect to his debt in obligations, his profit in supererogatory acts and virtues—his loss is disobedience. The suitable time for this commerce is the whole day. The treatment of his 'commanding soul' (*al-nafs al-ammāra*) must be severe.[A] He must first settle his account with it regarding the obligatory acts (*farā'id*). If he has performed them properly, he thanks God for it and increases its desirability for the soul. If he did not perform [the obligatory acts] at all, then he obliges [the soul] to make up for them. If he had performed them incompletely, then he forces upon it the charge of supererogatory duties. Now, in the case of a commission of sin, he concentrates on [the soul's] punishment, torment and censure, that it may fully rectify the excess—as the merchant does with his associate.

Just as he scrutinizes the mundane accounting of every measure and weight, so he records entries for gains and losses in order to preclude cheating. Thus, he must guard against the deceit and cunning of the soul. For it is deceptive, dubious and cunning. Therefore, let him first ask [the soul] to rectify the response to everything uttered in the course of his day; and let him make his soul liable for what account another will own at the high plateau of the Resurrection.

And the same holds with respect to what he has seen; indeed his notions, ideas, thoughts, standing, sitting, eating, drinking and sleeping—even his silence. For what reason was he silent, and why was he at rest?

If he knows all of the soul's obligations and proves his worth, performing his duty therewith, this worth is counted as his.

[A] The Qur'ān refers to the soul in different ways; *al-nafs al-ammāra bi'l-sū'* appears in verse XII.53. In discussions of the soul, *al-nafs al-ammāra bi'l-sū'* is very often contrasted to two higher states of soul: *al-nafs al-muṭma'inna* and *al-nafs al-rāḍiya*.

Therefore, the remainder of what is incumbent on him becomes manifest to him. Let him consolidate this in his soul and write it on the parchment of his heart, just as he wrote the remainder [of the commerce] owed by his associate, in both his memory and ledger.

The soul is a debtor whose debts must be paid in full, some of them in reparation and security; some in restitution in kind; and some by punishment. None of this is possible save after the account has been confirmed and what remains is determined truthfully in the obligatory manner. Upon that, one may turn to calling to account and demanding payment. Then, one must call the soul to account for every day and hour, through an entire lifetime and with respect to every organ, both exterior and interior—as narrated about Tawba b. Ṣumma, who lived in Riqqah.[A] He used to take his soul to account. One day he counted his age.[17] When he found he was sixty years old, he counted the days. When [he found] them to be one thousand five hundred and twenty-one days, he shouted, 'Woe to me, I shall meet the angel with a thousand five hundred and twenty-one days' misdeeds.[18] And every day ten thousand misdeeds there are!' Then he dropped on the spot and died. A voice was heard saying, 'With what speed to the highest paradise.'[19]

This is how every hour one must examine one's own soul for every breath and every disobedience[20] of the heart or the members. If the servant were to throw a stone into his house for every act of disobedience, he would fill his house within a short period of his life. But he is careless with his record of sins—although the two angels record [all] this for him. *God has reckoned it, though it be forgotten.*[21]

[A] A region in north-western Mesopotamia (Zabīdī 114).

CHAPTER FOUR

# The Fourth Steadfast Commitment: Punishing the Soul for Its Dereliction

HOWEVER MUCH GOD'S SERVANT examines his soul, it will be free neither of the temptation to sin nor of being remiss in respect of God's right. Therefore, he must not neglect [his soul]. Neglecting it facilitates his temptation to sin, to which his soul may grow accustomed and then find it difficult to shed it. This is what causes the ruin of the soul.[1] Indeed, he must punish it.

Should the servant eat a morsel on account of the soul's dubious appetite, he must punish the stomach with hunger. If he looks at a female who is not of marriageable [status], he must[2] amerce the eye by forbidding the gaze. This is how he may punish every part of his body—by denying himself his desires. This is the custom of those who take the way of the Hereafter.

Manṣūr b. Ibrāhīm relates that a worshipper speaking to a woman kept placing his hand on her thigh then became remorseful, so he put his hand over the fire until it was desiccated.[3]

It is related that a man among the Children of Israel used to worship at his hermitage. He did this for a long time. One particular day, while looking out, he saw a woman. Charmed and captivated by her, he stepped his foot forward to approach her, but God reminded him of a previous offence and he muttered, 'What is this that I wish to do?' Regaining himself and restrained by God, he felt remorseful. When he wanted to place his foot back into the hermitage, he said, 'How wrong, how wrong! Can a foot that moved forward intending to disobey God return with me to my hermitage? By God, never shall this come to pass!' He left his foot outside[4] the hermitage, scourged by rain, wind, ice, sun—until it was severed and fell off. God commended him for this and mentioned him in one of His books.

Junayd related that he heard Ibn al-Kartanī[5] say, 'I found myself impure one night and had to[6] perform the ritual wash. But the night was cold and I found myself tardy and slack. My soul murmured laxity to me until the morning when I can heat the water, or enter the bath and not weary myself.[7] I said, "How strange! I deal with God all my life, bound by His right over me;[8] yet I feel no haste inside me, only pause and slackness." I resolved to wash only with this patched garment on me. I resolved that I shall never remove, wring and dry it in the sun.'

It is told that when Ghazwān and Abū Mūsā [al-Ashʿarī] went on one of their military expeditions, a servant-girl was discovered. Ghazwānī looked at her, then lifted his hand and struck his eye until it jutted out.[9] He said, 'Because of the eye you were in harm's way.'

A man cast but one look at a woman and vowed never to drink cool water for the rest of his life. He drank lukewarm water to make life joyless.

It is told that Ḥassān b. Abī Sunān, passing by a dwelling, muttered, 'When was this built?' He addressed his soul, 'You ask about what concerns you not. I shall punish you with a year of fasting.' And he forced it to fast.[10]

Said Mālik b. Ḍaygham, 'Ribāḥ al-Qaysī came asking about my father after the afternoon prayer. We told him he was asleep. He said, "Sleep at this hour?[11] This is a time for sleep? Then I must leave." So we dispatched a messenger after him to tell him, "Should we wake him for you?"

'The messenger returned and said, "He was too occupied to understand anything from me. I reached him as he entered the cemetery, reproving[12] himself, 'Did you really say, is this hour a time for sleep? Is it up to you? Let the man sleep as he likes. What caused you to think that this was not an hour for sleep? You speak about what you know not. Verily, to God I make a vow, which I shall never break, that you will never lie on the ground to sleep except for a crippling illness or a swoon. Shame on you. Have you no shame? How you have been rebuked! There is no end to your transgression.' [The messenger] said, "The man began to weep without noticing my presence. When I saw this, I left him alone."'[13]

It is related that[14] Tamīm al-Dārī slept one night without rising for the night vigil. So he spent a whole year without sleep as punishment for what happened.

Ṭalḥa related that a man rushed off, removed his clothes and tossed himself in the hot sand, saying to himself, 'Taste, for Hell is even hotter. Are you cadaverous at night, sinful by day?' While doing this, he suddenly saw the Prophet (may God bless him and grant him peace) in the shade of a tree. He went to him and said, 'My soul has overpowered me.'

The Prophet asked him, 'Was it necessary to do what you did? The gates of Heaven shall be opened for you and God shall take pride in you with the angels.' The Prophet then said to his Companions, 'Learn from your brother.'

[Each of the Companions] took to saying, 'O so-and-so, pray for me.'[15] The Prophet said, 'Include them!'

'O Lord, make piety their provision, make righteous their affairs,' said the man.

The Prophet then said 'Lord, guide him [to the best prayer]...' and the man said, 'Lord, make paradise their place of return.'[16]

Said Ḥudhayfa b. Qatāda, 'A man was asked, "What do you do with your soul's desires?" "No soul on the face of the earth is more loathsome to me," he said. "How can I then give it its desires?"'[17]

Ibn al-Sammāk entered upon Dā'ūd al-Ṭā'ī after the latter had died and while [his body] was still on the ground in his house. He said, 'O Dā'ūd, you imprisoned your soul before it became imprisoned. You tormented it before it became tormented. And today you shall see the reward of the One for whom you acted.'[18]

Wahb b. Munabbih [al-Yamānī] related that a man prayed for a [long] time. Then a need arose in him for something from God. So he fasted every Saturday for seventy Saturdays, eating eleven dates [only] in each. Then he asked for what he needed[19] but he was not granted it. He returned to his soul, saying, 'I will do away with you. If you had some good in you, you would have been granted your desire.' An angel descended upon him and said, 'O son of Adam, this hour of yours [reproaching your soul] is better than your past worship. God hath granted your desire.'[20]

Said ᶜAbd Allāh b. Qays,[A] 'We were on a military expedition when the enemy appeared. The alert was made and everyone stood in rank; it was a very windy day. A man in front of me addressed himself, "O my soul, was I not at such-and-such a battle and you said to me, 'What of your family and children?' and I obeyed you and retreated? Was I not at such-and-such a battle and you said to me, 'What of your family and children?' and I obeyed you and retreated? By God, I shall present thee before God today, either He will take you or He will let you live."

'I said I would watch him that day, and I watched him. When the mass [of soldiers] attacked their enemy, he was in the forefront. Then the enemy attacked, and the soldiers were exposed. He remained where he was until they were exposed several times, standing his ground and fighting. By God, he continued in this and persevered until I saw him thrown to the ground. I counted in him and his mount sixty or more gashes.'

We have already mentioned the tradition [transmitted] about Abū Ṭalḥa when he was distracted from his prayer by a bird in his walled enclosure;[21] in penance he divested himself of the walled enclosure as alms. And that ᶜUmar used to strike his feet with a scourge every night and say, 'What have you wrought today?'

Mujammaᶜ related that once he lifted his head to a roof terrace

[A] That is, Abū Mūsā al-Ashᶜarī.

and his eyes fell upon a woman. He vowed never to lift his head towards the sky as long as he lived in this world.

At night, al-Aḥnaf b. Qays [al-Tamīmī] ever had a lantern beside him. He used to place his finger over it and say to himself, 'What compelled you to do this on such-and-such a day?'

Wahīb b. al-Ward denied himself something[A] and plucked out the hairs of his chest until the pain was great. Then he took to telling himself, 'I want only the best for you.'[22]

Muḥammad b. Bishr once saw Dā'ūd al-Ṭā'ī eating unsalted bread for breakfast. He said to him, 'What if you ate it with salt?'

[Dā'ūd] replied, 'My soul has been urging me for a year [to eat] salt,' but Dā'ūd tasted no more salt as long as he lived in this world.[23]

This, then, is how those who possess resolve (*ulī al-ʿazm*) punish themselves. What is remarkable is that you should punish your servant, community, household and child for what they do out of character and for being remiss in something; you fear that if you let them off, they would not obey your choice and would turn on you. And yet, you neglect your soul, your worst enemy and worst oppressor. The harm from its oppression is greater than the harm of your household, since their goal is merely to disturb your life in this world.

If you are discerning, you would know that living is living for the Hereafter, where the abiding comfort has no end. Your soul is what spoils the life of the Hereafter. It is the first to be punished before anything else.

[A] As a form of discipline.

## CHAPTER FIVE

# The Fifth Steadfast Commitment: Renewed Striving

THE FACT IS THAT WHEN A PERSON examines his soul, he finds it tempted by sin. Therefore, he must punish it in the manners described above. If he finds it sapless to the point of sloth with respect to anything to do with virtue and private devotion (*awrād*), he must discipline it by taxing it with [more] devotions and a variety of tasks, both on account of its omission and to compensate for what it has already been remiss in. This is how those who labour for God behave.

Having missed the public afternoon prayer, ʿUmar b. al-Khaṭṭāb (may God be pleased with him) punished himself by giving in alms land that belonged to him worth a hundred thousand dirhams.

Whenever Ibn ʿUmar missed a public prayer he spent the same night in prayer. One night, he delayed the sunset prayer until two stars appeared [in the night sky].[A] For this he manumitted two slaves.

When [al-Ḥarth b. ʿAbd Allāh] Ibn Abī Rabīʿa missed the two *rakʿa*s of the morning prayer, he manumitted a slave.

Another man used to impose a year's fasting on himself, go on the pilgrimage on foot or give away all his money in alms. All this comprises the steadfast commitment (*murābaṭa*) and censure of the soul for its own salvation.

You may argue: If my soul does not comply with me regarding

[A] Meaning he missed the prayer.

renewed striving (*mujāhada*) and assiduity in private devotions, how should it be treated?

I say: The way is to let the soul hear what the reports say about those who strove [in the way of God] (*mujtahidūn*). The most useful treatment is to associate with one of God's servants who is striving in worship, to heed his words and to emulate him. As one man used to say, 'When languor in worship disgraces me, I observe the case of Muḥammad b. Wāsiʿ and his striving and act thus for a week.' However, this treatment is impracticable, since nowadays no one is as striving in worship as were the ancients. Therefore, one must turn from observing to hearing (*samāʿ*). And nothing is more useful than hearing about them and perusing their reports. Those who have given their utmost (*al-juhd al-jahīd*), whose toil has come to an end and whose reward and ease shall last forever without interruption—what greater dominion is there than theirs? There can be no greater regret than that of he who does not emulate them, gratifying his soul [instead] with troubling desires for a paltry few days, and then death takes him away and he is forever barred from whatever he coveted? God protect us from this!

We shall adduce some descriptions and virtues of those who strive (*mujtahidīn*) so as to cause the seeker to desire striving (*ijtihād*) in imitation of them.

Said the Messenger of God (may God bless him and grant him peace), 'God bless a people whom others thought ill, but they are not ill.'[1] Al-Ḥasan [al-Baṣrī] said [in explanation], 'Worship had worn them out (*ajhadathum al-ʿibāda*).'

God said, *And those who give what they give with fearful hearts*.[2] Al-Ḥasan explained that they act piously as they do because they fear that this may not save them from God's punishment.[3]

Said the Messenger of God, 'Blessed is he who lives long and acts well.'[4]

It is related that God Exalted asked His angels, 'Why do my servants strive?' They said, 'Our Lord, you fill them with fear about something and they are frightened—you make them long for something and they long for it.'[A] And God said, 'What if my servants should see Me? They would strive even more.'[5]

Said al-Ḥasan, 'I have known people and befriended some who neither rejoice in nor regret anything of this world; it is more worthless in their eyes[6] than this dust you tread upon with your feet. Each of them could live out his life without a gown to wrap himself with and without ever ordering his household to prepare food or putting anything between himself and the ground.[B] I realised that they act according to the book of their Lord and the way of their Prophet. When night falls upon them, they rise to their feet and lay down their faces,[C] and tears run down their cheeks, whispering to their Lord to spare them. Whenever they do a good deed, they rejoice and eagerly give thanks for it, asking God to accept it. They grieve whenever they commit a misdeed and ask God to forgive them what they did. By God, they persist in this. By God, they were not free of sin, nor were they saved but through pardon.'[7]

It is told that while people were visiting ʿUmar b. ʿAbd al-ʿAzīz during his illness a gaunt youth was present. ʿUmar asked him, 'Young lad, what has brought upon you what I see?' The young man said, 'O Commander of the Faithful, sickness and disease.'

'I seek honesty from you,' said ʿUmar.

'O Commander of the Faithful, I tasted the sweetness of this world and found it bitter. Its glitter and sweetness are insignificant to me; its gold and granite are of equal value. It is as if I were gazing at my Lord's throne while people drive towards Paradise and Hell. Therefore, I go thirsty by day and sleepless by night. Everything I do is meagre and puny beside the reward and punishment of God.'[8]

Abū Nuʿaym stated that Dāʾūd al-Ṭāʾī used to drink bread in

[A] This refers to the fear of Hell and the longing for Paradise.

[B] For bedding.

[C] Meaning that while others lie down at night, they rise up and then prostrate themselves.

water instead of just eating bread. When asked about this, he said, '[The difference in time] between chewing bread and drinking bread soup is the recitation of fifty Qur'ānic verses.'[9]

One day a man came to him and said, 'The roof of your house has a broken beam.' He replied, 'O my brother's son, I have not had to look at the roof of this house for twenty years.' They disliked[10] wasteful gazing as much as they did prattle.[11]

Said Muḥammad b. ʿAbd al-ʿAzīz, 'We sat with Aḥmad b. al-Rizzīn from morning to afternoon. He was oblivious of everything to his right and to his left. Asked about this, he said, "God Almighty and Majestic created the two eyes of the servant for beholding God's majesty. Against him who looks on without reflection a sin is recorded."'

Said the wife of Masrūq, 'Masrūq's feet were always swollen because of the length of his prayers.' She said, 'By God, I used to sit behind him and weep out of pity for him!''

Said Abū Dardā', 'I would desire not a single day of life if not for three things: thirsting at midday for God, prostrating before God in the middle of the night and sitting with people who select the best of words just as one selects the best of fruits.'[12]

Al-Aswad b. Yazīd used to persevere in worship and to fast in the heat until his body turned green and yellow.[A] ʿUlquma b. Qays asked him, 'Why do you torment your soul?'

'I seek its honour,' he answered.[13]

He used to fast until his body turned green and to pray until he dropped. Then Anas b. Mālik and al-Ḥasan [al-Baṣrī] came to him. They said to him, 'God Almighty and Majestic has not commanded you to do all this.'

He replied,[14] 'I am a servant, owned [by God]. I do not claim to be humble without being so.'

One of those who strive prayed a thousand *rakʿas* a day until his legs gave way. Seated, he then prayed a thousand more *rakʿas*. Performing the afternoon prayers, he sat with his legs drawn and

[A] That is, waned and weakened.

then said, 'How strange that human beings should ask of Thee other than Thee! How strange that they should take comfort in other than Thee; indeed that their hearts should be lit up by remembrance of other than Thee.'

Thābit al-Bunānī loved[15] prayer and used to say, 'Lord, if You permit anyone to pray (*ṣalāt*) to You from his grave, then permit me to pray from my grave.'[16]

Said Junayd, 'I know of no one more devoted to worship than Sarī [al-Saqaṭī]. Having lived ninety-eight years, he was seen lying down only at death.'[17]

Said Ḥārith b. Saʿd, 'Some people came upon a monk and saw what he had done to himself with intense striving. They questioned him about this and he said, "This is nothing like the horrors that people shall see and of which they are ignorant. They devote themselves to no more than their portions [in this world],[18] forgetting their greatest portion [that lies] with their Lord." The people then wept, one and all.'

On the authority of Abū Muḥammad al-Mughāzilī, it is said that Abū Muḥammad al-Jarīrī had gone to Mecca one year. He neither slept nor spoke; leaned on neither a pillar nor a wall; and never stretched out his legs. Abū Bakr al-Kattānī passed by him [one day]. He greeted him, saying,[19] 'O Muḥammad, how are you capable of such devotion?'

He answered, '[God] knows my inner truthfulness and He supports me in my outer.' Al-Kattānī bowed and turned away in reflection.

A man[A] once said, 'I went to see Fatḥ al-Mawṣilī and saw he had his palms out-stretched. He was weeping and, I noticed, tears dripped from his fingers. When I approached him, his tears had a reddish tinge. I said, "By God, do you weep blood, O Fatḥ?"

'He replied, "Had you not entreated me by God, I would not have told you. Yes, I weep blood."

'So I asked him, "For what reason do you shed tears?"

[A] Namely, Abū Ismāʿīl—one of Fatḥ's companions (Zabīdī 124).

'He replied, "[I weep] for attending tardily to the duty of God's right. And I weep tears of blood lest my tears [alone] be in vain." After he died I saw him in a dream and asked him, "How has God treated you?"

'"He forgave me."

'"What did He make of your tears?"

'"My Lord, Mighty and Majestic, drew me near and asked me, 'O Fatḥ, why the tears?' I said, 'Lord, for failing to attend to the duty of Thy right.' 'What about the blood?'—He asked. 'Because my tears might not be allotted to me.' He said to me, 'O Fatḥ, what do you intend by all this? By My power and majesty, your two caretaker angels[A] have kept your record for forty years and it has no fault.'"'

It is told that, as they set out on a journey, some people deviated from the path and came across a reclusive monk. They called out to him. He looked down upon them from his hermitage. They said, 'O monk, we have lost our way. What is the way?' He motioned with his head to the sky. The people understood what he meant and said, 'Monk, we beseech you, will you answer us?'

'Ask, but not too much. For the day shall never return, nor life be repeated, and the seeker is quick [to seek].'

The people were bewildered by what he said. They asked, 'Monk, how will people fare on the morrow with their Lord?'[B]

'Depending on their intentions,' he said.

'Advise us,' they pleaded.

'Take provisions in proportion to your journey. The best provision is what achieves the purpose.' He led them to the path then betook himself to his hermitage.

Said ʿAbd al-Wāḥid b. Zayd [al-Baṣrī], 'I came to the hermitage of one of the monks of China and called him, "O monk," but he did not answer. I called a second time. No answer. And a third time. He then looked down upon me and said, "O man, I am

[A] The angels that record one's good deeds and one's sins.

[B] That is, how will people fare with God on the Day of Judgement.

no monk. A monk is someone who is frightened of God[A] in His heaven and aggrandises Him in His glory; who is forbearing when God afflicts him; who is satisfied with His decree; who praises Him for His blessings; who thanks Him for His bounties; who is humbled by His greatness and subdued by His might; who yields in awe of Him; who thinks about His reckoning and punishment. He fasts by day and holds vigil by night. Thoughts of the Fire and the questioning by the Almighty keep him awake. That is the monk. I am but a rapacious dog. I have imprisoned myself in this hermitage away from people in order not to perturb them."

'I asked him, "Monk, what separates people from God after[20] they had known Him?"

'"Brother, only the love for this world and its glitter separates people from God. This is because [the world] is a place of sins and crimes. The sensible man casts it from his heart. He turns to God in repentance for his crime and accepts what brings him closer to his Lord."'[21]

Dā'ūd al-Ṭā'ī was told, 'If only you combed your whiskers.' He answered, 'But then I would be idle.'[22]

Uways [b. ʿĀmir] al-Qaranī used to say, 'This is a night for kneeling,' and he would kneel [in prayer] all night. The next night, he used to say, 'This is a night for prostration.' And he would spend the whole night in prostration.[23]

It is told that when ʿUtba [b. Abān] al-Ghulām turned [to God in repentance], he ceased to enjoy eating and drinking. His mother then told him, 'If only you were kind to yourself.' He said, 'Kindness is what I desire. Leave me to a little hardship for much ease.'[24]

Masrūq went on the pilgrimage and when he slept it was only in [ritual] prostration.[25]

Said Sufyān al-Thawrī, 'In the morning, the people of secrecy[B] are praised and at death the people of devoutness.'[26]

[A] *Rāhib* (monk) and *rahaba* (to fear), a play on words.

[B] Meaning those who rise in the secrecy of night for worship.

Said ᶜAbd Allāh b. Dā'ūd [al-Hamdānī], 'When any of them reached forty years old, he folded up his blanket—that is, he did not sleep the whole night.'

And Abū al-Ḥasan Kahmas b. al-Ḥasan used to perform a thousand cycles [of prayer] every day and say to himself, 'Get up, O Ye shelter for every evil.' When he became weak, he limited himself to five hundred cycles [of prayer] and used to cry out, 'Half of my work gone.'[27]

The daughter of al-Rabīᶜ b. Khuthaym used to ask him, 'O my father, why is it that I see people sleeping but you do not sleep?'

'O my daughter, your father fears slumber,'[A] he said.[28]

When al-Rabīᶜ's mother saw how much he wept and remained sleepless, she asked him, 'O my son, have you perchance slain someone?'

'Yes, my mother.'

'Who is he that we may search for his family to grant you forgiveness. By God, if they only knew how you are now, they would surely be merciful and forgive you!'

'It is my own self, O mother.'[29]

Said [Abū Ḥafṣ] ᶜUmar, the nephew of Bishr b. al-Ḥārith [al-Ḥāfī], 'I heard my uncle Bishr b. al-Ḥarith[30] say to my mother, "Sister, my abdomen and my sides assail me." My mother said to him, "Brother, permit me to recommend you some broth with a handful of flour I have. Drinking it will improve your insides."

'He said to her while rubbing himself, "I fear being asked where I have obtained this flour and knowing not what to say." My mother wept, he wept and I wept with them.'

And ᶜUmar said, 'My mother found Bishr in intense pain. He began to breath weakly. She told him, "Brother, I wish your mother had not given birth to me. By God, my liver is torn to pieces[B] for [the state] I find you in."'[31]

[A] Meaning that death may come to him while he is unprepared.

[B] In Arabic, the liver, as well as the heart, is the seat of emotions. 'My liver is torn to pieces' is the equivalent of saying 'My heart is breaking.'

'I heard him tell her, "And I wish my mother had not given birth to me—and if she did, that her breasts had not granted me milk."' ʿUmar added that his mother used to weep for him day and night.

Al-Rabīʿ said that he went to Uways and found him seated, having performed the morning prayer. 'And he sat and I sat, saying [to myself ] that I will not distract him from the rosary.[A] He remained in his place until the noon prayer. Then he rose for the afternoon prayer. He later sat down until the sunset prayer and stayed in his place to perform the night prayer. He remained seated there for the morning prayer. Then his eyes prevailed upon him and he said, "Lord, I seek refuge in Thee from the sleepy eye and the insatiable stomach." So I said, "This suffices for me from him," and I returned'.

Looking at Uways, a man once said, 'O ʿAbd Allāh, why do you seem ill?' He answered, 'How could Uways not be ill? The sick are fed but Uways does not eat. The sick sleep but Uways does not.'

Said Aḥmad b. Ḥarb, 'How odd for someone who knows that Paradise stands adorned above him and that Hellfire is kindled below him—how could he sleep between them.'

One of the ascetics once said, 'I went to Ibrāhīm b. Adham and found him performing the night prayer, so I sat down in wait. He wrapped himself in a woollen cloak and laid himself down. He never turned from one side to the other once until morning broke. Then, the muezzin began his call to prayer, and [Ibrāhīm] sprang up to pray without having done his ablutions. This burrowed into my breast. I told him, "God be merciful upon you. You slept, recumbent, the entire night without thereafter renewing your ablutions!"[B]

'He answered, "The whole night I roamed sometimes the

[A] Use of the rosary may follow the regular prayer.

[B] It is compulsory to renew one's ablutions if one has slept and in particular if one has slept lying down.

gardens of Paradise, sometimes the gorges of Hellfire. Is there sleep in this?"'

Said Thābit al-Bunānī, 'I saw two men, one of whom prayed and could reach his bed only by crawling.'[32]

It is said that Abū Bakr b. ʿAyyāsh never once lay on his side on a bed in forty years. He developed a cataract in one eye, but for twenty years his family knew nothing of it.

It is said that Samnūn [b. Ḥamza] used to perform five hundred cycles of prayer every day.[33]

And Abū Bakr al-Muṭawwaʿī said, 'In my youth, my private devotion every[34] day and night was to recite the verse *Say: He is God, the one and only*[35] thirty-one or forty thousand times'—though this is doubted by the transmitter.

If you saw Manṣūr b. al-Muʿtamar, you would say he was a man afflicted with misfortune, crippled of limb, muffled of voice, moist of eyes. If you stirred him, his eyes would appear as four.[A] His mother asked him, 'What have you done to yourself? You cry the whole night without stop. Have you injured someone, have you killed anyone?'

'O mother,' he said, 'I best know what I have done with myself.'[36]

ʿĀmir b. ʿAbd Allāh was asked, 'How patient are you with the night vigil and with thirst at the midday heat?'

He replied, 'Have I not deferred the day's meal to the night, and the night's slumber to the day? There is nothing great here.'

He used to say, 'I have found nothing like Paradise, he who seeks it slumbers; I have found nothing like Hell, he who wishes to escape it slumbers.'[B] At nightfall, he would said, 'The heat of the Fire takes away sleep'. He did not sleep until morning's rising. When day arrived he would said, 'The heat of the Fire takes away sleep,' and he became emaciated for lack of sleep. When night fell

[A] That is, he was weeping and the tears were coming out of both sides of each eye making it appear as if he had four weeping eyes.

[B] Meaning that he is surprised that those who seek Paradise should slumber and those who fear Hell should slumber.

he would said, 'He goes forth who is fearful.' In the morning, he praised the people of secrecy.[37]

A man used to say, 'Having accompanied ʿĀmir b. ʿAbd al-Qays for four months, I never saw him sleep either by day or by night.'[38]

It is told that a companion of Alī b. Abī Ṭālib's once said, 'I performed the morning prayer behind ʿAlī. When he finished the prayer, he turned to his left in distress and remained there until sunrise. Then he turned his hands over[A] and said, "By God, I saw [with my own eyes] Muḥammad's Companions. [Alas,] today I see no one like them. They used to rise in the morning dishevelled, dusty and pale, after spending the night for God prostrated and standing and reciting God's Book, and alternating between their feet and their foreheads. When they invoked God they quivered[39] as the tree quivers on a windy day. Their eyes shed tears that soaked their clothes. It is as if people are unaware!"' Meaning those around him now.[40]

Abū Muslim [ʿAbd Allāh b. Thawbat] al-Khawlānī hung a whip in his place of worship at home in order to fill himself with fear. He used to say to his soul, 'Rise! By God, I shall move forward despite thee, until the weariness is thine, not mine.' And when languor came, he grabbed his whip and struck his thigh with it, 'You are more deserving of a lashing than my mule.'[41]

He said, 'Do Muḥammad's Companions think that they will have him to themselves without us? No, by God, we will jostle them hard[42] for [proximity to] him that they may know they have left behind them those who are worthy.'

Ṣafwān b. Salīm's thighs became stiff from standing too long [in prayer]. His reasoning was that had he been told that the Day of Judgement would be tomorrow, he would not have been able to find more to do.

When winter set in, he used to lay on the roof that the cold may afflict him. In summer, he slept inside houses that the heat

[A] A gesture of distress.

may keep him from sleeping. He died in prostration.[43] And he used to say, 'Lord, I long to meet Thee and so long to meet me.'

Said al-Qāsim b. Muḥammad, 'I went out one morning. It was my habit whenever I went out to go first to greet ʿĀ'isha. That day, I went to her and she was performing her forenoon prayer and she was reciting, *But God granted us favour and protected us from the scorching wind.*[44] She wept, supplicated and repeated the verse. I stood there until I wearied, while she remained as she was. When I saw this, I went to the market. I told myself I would finish my chore and return. I finished my chore and returned but she was the same. She repeated the verse, wept and supplicated.'[45]

Muḥammad b. Isḥāq recounted that when ʿAbd al-Raḥmān b. al-Aswad arrived as a pilgrim, he was hurt in one foot. So, he prayed on one foot. And the morning prayer he performed with the previous night's ablution.[A46]

One man said, 'My fear of death is only that it might keep me from the night prayer.'

Said ʿAlī b. Abī Ṭālib, 'The righteous (*ṣāliḥūn*) usually have a pale complexion from sleeplessness, their eyes bleary from weeping, their lips withered from fasting and upon them lies the dust of the meek.'[47]

Al-Ḥasan al-Baṣrī was asked, 'Why are those who keep the night vigil best?' 'Because they are alone with the Merciful. He envelops them with a light from Him. He clothes them with His light.'[48]

And ʿĀmir b. ʿAbd al-Qays [al-ʿAnbar al-Baṣrī] used to say, 'Lord, you created me without consulting me; you take my life away without apprising me; you created with me a foe, who is second nature to me and who sees me but I do not see him.[B] Then you ask me to restrain myself. Lord, how can I be restrained if you do not restrain me? Lord, this world has only worries and pains. The Hereafter has the penalty and the account. So, where is the repose and the joy?'[49]

[A] Suggesting that he prayed all night.

[B] Referring to his soul.

Jaʿfar b. Muḥammad said that ʿUtba [b. Abān] al-Ghulām used to pass the night with three cries. After praying the night prayer he would place his head between his knees in thought. After spending a third of the night, he would let out a cry and place his head between his knees in thought. When the second third of the night was over, he let out a cry and place his head between his knees in thought. At predawn, he would let out a cry. Jaʿfar b. Muḥammad said that he asked someone from Baṣra about this. 'Do not bother with his crying, but rather with what has—between cries—led him to cry out.'[50]

It is told that al-Qāsim b. Rāshid al-Shaybānī said that Zumʿa was accompanying us to al-Muḥaṣṣab.[A] With him were wife and daughters. He prayed for a lengthy night. At predawn, he called out at the top of his voice, 'O ye, married travelling companions, will you sleep all the night? Will you not rise and wander about?' They sprung up. And then he heard those who wept here, a supplicator there, a reciter here and someone doing ablutions there. When morning arrived, he called out at the top of his voice—in the morning did he praise the people of secrecy.

A learned person once said, 'God has servants upon whom He bestows his blessing and who acknowledge Him. He broadened their hearts and they obey Him. They rely upon Him and submit creation and [every] matter [alike] to Him. Their hearts are the sources of limpid certainty, houses of wisdom, coffers of grandeur, treasures of power. They come and go among people, yet their hearts rove the realm of the heavenly kingdom, taking shelter in the veil of the invisible, and then return with rarities[51] of gainful subtleties. No one can describe it. In their interior, they are like comely brocade; in their exterior, like kerchiefs offered to one desiring their humility. This state is inaccessible through striving, but as a favour from God, one bestowed upon whomever He wishes.'

[A] A place near Mecca (Zabīdī 132).

A righteous man said, 'While travelling in the hills of Jerusalem I descended into a valley and suddenly a voice rang out. The voice carried well in those hills. I followed it and came upon a garden[52] with trees all round. A man stood in it repeating this [Qur'ānic] phrase,[53] *On the day when every soul shall be confronted with what good it has wrought...but God cautions you about Himself.*[54] I sat behind him to listen to his words as he repeated this verse, when he suddenly let out a cry and fell in a swoon.[55]

'I said, "What a pity! This pains me." And I awaited his recovery.

'He recovered after an hour and I heard him say, "I seek Thy protection from the station of the deniers. I seek Thy protection from the deeds of the untrue. I seek Thy protection from the shunning of the heedless." Then he said, "Before Thee are humbled the hearts of the fearful and to Thee flee the hopes of the slack. Humbled are the hearts of the cognisant (*ʿārifūn*) before Thy greatness."

'Dusting off his hands, he said,[56] "What have I to do with this world? And what has this world to do with me? O world, have thy kin and those accustomed to thy comforts. Go to your intimates. Deceive them!" Then he said, "Where have the past generations and those who lived aforetime gone? They are put to the test in the dust, and in time they perish."

'So, I called out to him, "O servant of God, I have been standing behind you all day waiting for you to become free."

'He replied, "How can one be free who is assailed by time and whom time hastens on—who fears death may overtake him? Or, how can anyone be free whose days are gone but whose sins remain?" Then he said,[57] "It's up to you. I anticipate every hardship." He then turned away from me for an hour. And he recited, *And God shall confront them with something they could never reckon.*[58]

'He cried out once again, louder than the first time, and fell in a swoon. I thought he had surely given up the ghost. I approached him while he was agitated. Recovering, he said, "Who am I? What has happened to me? Please[59] grant me my sins.[A] Honour me with Thy veil. Efface my offences with the dignity of Thy face when I stand before Thee."

'I told him, "I urge you by the One whom you hope from and upon whom you rely, to speak to me."

'He replied, "Take the words of he whose words benefit you and shun the words of the one debased by his sins. Since God has willed it, I have been here fighting Iblīs and he fights me. He found nothing to help him draw me away from where I was except you—so be gone, O Deceived One! You have stopped my tongue [from remembering God] and part of my heart tilted towards your utterance. I seek refuge in God from your evil. I wish He would spare me His displeasure and grace me with His mercy."'

The [narrator] finally said [to himself], 'I shall not distract this friend of God for fear of punishment on the very spot on which I stand. I turned away and left him.'

A righteous man said, 'While travelling on one of my journeys, I turned to rest beneath a tree. Suddenly I found an old man looking at me. He said, "O man, get up! For death dies not." He then wandered about and I followed him. I listened to him as he said, "*Every soul shall taste death*[60]—Lord give me Thy blessings in death."

'I added for him[61] "and beyond death."

'He said, "He who is certain about what is beyond death readies the cover of prudence.[62] He has nothing in this world that endures." And he said, "O Ye to whose Face every face offers itself, whiten my face with a gaze upon Thee. Fill my heart with love for Thee. Protect me from the ignominy of[63] Your rebuke on the morrow. It is about time that I should be ashamed in front of Thee. It is about time that I turn back from avoidance of Thee."

'He also said, "Without Your clemency, my years would not be enough for me.[B] Without Your pardon, my hope would not

[A] That is, 'God, free me of my sins.'

[B] That is, if not for the clemency of God a lifespan would not be enough to reach a good end.

extend to what is with Thee." Then he departed and left me.'

> This meaning has been emphasized in:
> Emaciated of body, heavy of heart,
> at Qunna,[64] valley's bottom, ye shall find him.
> Bemoaning sins and disgraces,
> Their gravity roiling sweet slumber.
> His fears astir and growing,
> he calls out, 'Succour me, O my support!
> for Ye knoweth well my encounters,
> ever lenient with people's oversights.'

It is also said:

> Sweeter than the delight in beautiful women
> as they flush in comely dress...
> So the contrite one flees kith and wealth,
> roves from place to place,
> To be forgotten, to be alone,
> in worship to triumph as he desires[65]
> His pleasure—recital wherever a master he finds,
> and remembrance through the heart and the tongue.
> Upon death a herald to him comes
> to announce deliverance from disgrace.
> Then he fathoms what comforts he wanted and desired
> in the chambers of the heart.[66]

Kariz b. Wubra[67] used to recite the whole Qur'ān thrice every day. In worship he was as diligent as can be and was told, 'You exert yourself in worship.'

He answered, 'What is the world's duration?'

'Seven thousand years,' he was told.

'How long is the Day of Resurrection?'[68] he asked.

'Fifty thousand years.'

'How can anyone of you then fail to strive seven days to secure that Day?'

In other words, if you lived the duration of the world, strove for seven thousand years and were saved from [the terrors of] a single day lasting fifty thousand years, your gain would be great. And you would have been right in seeking this. But how short still your life and endless the Hereafter![69]

This is how the righteous forefathers lived in steadfast commitment and vigilance of the soul. Therefore, however recalcitrant your soul may be with you and averse to consistent worship, acquaint yourself with the states of [the righteous], for rare are those who resemble them today. If you can observe someone who takes them as a model, that person is healthiest of heart and inspires imitation best, because reporting is not like observing. If you are unable [to observe], then do not overlook learning about the states of [other people]. 'If it's not a camel, 'tis a goat'—choose for yourself between, on the one hand, their emulation and being in their midst and company, for they are discerning, wise, and have religious insight; and, on the other, emulating the ignorant and heedless of your age.

Hence, do not accept [your soul's] affiliation with the foolish or be content with comparison with dolts, giving preference to contradicting what intelligent people do. If your soul tells you the latter are powerful men who cannot be emulated, consider then the state of striving women and say to yourself, 'O soul, do not refrain from being weaker than women.' I belittle the man who is not equal to a woman either in her religion or mundane affairs.'

Let us now mention a snippet from the states of striving women (*mujāhidāt*). It is told that whenever Ḥabība al-ʿAdawiyya prayed in the night, she would do so[70] on a terrace that belonged to her, she would tighten her garment and veil and say, 'Lord, the stars have slipped away, the eyes fallen asleep; the kings have bolted their gates and every lover is alone with his beloved. This is my station between Your hands.' Then she turned to prayer. With the break of dawn, she said, 'Lord, the night has stolen away and this day waxes bright. I wish I knew if You accepted my night, for I would be delighted; or that you rejected it of me, for I would then be blameworthy. By your Majesty, ever shall I persist the remainder of my life. By your Majesty,[71] should you chase me away from Your gate,[72] I would not stir from the generosity and munificence You have shown me.'[73]

It is told that ʿUjra used to spend the night [in prayer]. She was sightless. At dawn she called with her grieving voice, 'Towards Thee do worshippers traverse the gloom of the nights, racing, racing to Thy mercy and to the blessing of Thy pardon. Therefore, Thee I ask, no one else, to make me foremost among those who race forth; to raise me towards Thee at the loftiest heights of those nearest You and to keep close to Your righteous servants. You are the most merciful of the merciful, greatest of the great, noblest of the noble, O Noble One.' She sank [to the ground] in prostration, which was heard [in Heaven], and she would go on supplicating and weeping until dawn.[74]

Said Yaḥyā b. Bisṭām, 'I used to take part in gatherings with Shaʿwāna. I saw how she mourned and wept. So I said to my companion, "If only we went to her while she is alone and commend her to be gentler with herself." He said, "Go to it!"

'So, we went to her and I told her, "If you were gentler with yourself and lessened your weeping a little, you would better attain what you want."

'She cried, then said, "By God, I wish to cry to the end of my tears, then to weep with blood until not a drop of blood is left in any of my members. I must weep, I must weep"—she kept repeating this until she fainted.'[75]

Muḥammad b. Muʿādh related that a devout woman told him, 'I dreamt that I was brought to Paradise. I saw the denizens of Paradise standing by its gates. I asked why the denizens of Paradise should be standing there. Someone replied, "They came out to behold this woman adorning the Gardens with her arrival."

'"And who is that woman?" I asked.

'"A black lady [of God] from the people of Abilla[76] called Shaʿwāna," came the reply. "My sister, by God!" I said.[A] As I

[A] This may mean a sister in God and not a blood sister.

said this, she was welcomed in on a stately camel flying in the air. When I saw her, I called out, "O sister, from your place do you not see my place? Pray for me that your Master might admit me with you."

'She smiled at me and said, "Your arrival is not due. But keep to two things I give you. Bring grief to bear upon your heart, prefer love for God to your [worldly] passions; and then whenever you die, it will not be to your detriment."'[77]

Said ʿAbd Allāh b. al-Ḥasan, 'I once had a Greek servant-girl. I used to admire her. One night, while she slept next to me, I woke to touch her,[78] but could not find her, so I rose [from bed] to look for her. She lay prostrated, saying, "By Thy love for me forgive my sins."

'I told her not to say "By Thy love for me" but "by my love for Thee."

'She said, "No, master. By His love for me He has taken me from polytheism to Islam. And by His love He opened my eyes—many of His people are asleep."'[79]

Said Abū Ḥāshim al-Qurashī,[80] 'A woman from the people of Yemen, said to be high-bred, arrived and went over to one of our homes. At night I heard her wailing and sobbing. One day I said to a woman servant of mine, "See what this woman is doing."' [Then,] he continued, 'The servant watched her and had found her doing nothing but gazing at the heavens while facing the *qibla*, and saying,[81] "You created a noblewoman, then provided her with your blessings from one situation to another. Every situation You [bestow upon] her has its goodness, every trial its beauty to her. Despite this she is exposed to Your wrath, being aware of disobedience to Thee, one slip at a time. Do You think her[82] unaware that You know of her evil deeds when You are the Omniscient and the All-aware?"'

Said Dhū al-Nūn al-Miṣrī, 'One night I was leaving the Valley of Canaan. I trekked up past the valley, when a dark figure drew towards me weeping and saying, *And God shall confront them with something they could never reckon.*[83] The dark figure approached and then, lo, it was a woman wearing a woollen garment and a pot in her hand. Unafraid of me, she said, "Who are you?"

'"An exile," said I.[84]

'"And is there exile with God, man?" she said.

'I wept at her words.

'She asked me, "What makes you weep?"

'"The remedy hit upon[85] a festering ailment, thus speeding its success."

'"But why should you cry if you are sincere?"

'"God's mercy on you! So the sincere should not weep?"

'"No."

'"Why not?"

'"Because weeping is rest for the heart." With these words, I fell silent.'[A]

Said Aḥmad b. ʿAlī, 'We sought Ghufayra's[86] permission to enter, but she hid from sight. We continued to wait by the door. When she learned of this, she rose to open it for us, and I heard her say, "Lord, I seek protection in Thee from the one who distracts me from Thy remembrance." With this she opened the door and we entered her house. We told her,[87] "O lady of God, pray for us."

'She said, "May God count your reception in my house as forgiveness." Then she said to us, "For forty years ʿAṭāʾ al-Sulamī never looked up to heaven. But he chanced to gaze upon it once. For that he fell into a swoon and was afflicted with hernia in his belly. If only Ghufayra[88] could raise her head without disobeying. If only she could disobey without repeating it."'[89]

A righteous man said, 'One day I went to the market with an Abyssinian servant-girl. I told her to keep to a spot near the market and left for a chore, telling her, "Do not leave until I attend to you."[90] When I returned I found she was not at the spot.

[A] The implication being that those who are sincere in their love do not rest.

I headed for my house infuriated with her. When she saw me she recognized the anger on my face.

'"O master, do not be hasty with me, for you sat me where I saw no one remembering God Exalted. I feared He would strike this place down." I was surprised by her words and declared to her, "You are free."

'She said, "What I did is bad. I used to serve you and claim two rewards. Now, one of them is gone."'[91]

Said Ibn ᶜAlā' al-Saᶜdī, 'I had a cousin called Burayra. She was devoutly observant and avidly read the Book.[A] When she came to a verse that mentioned Hellfire, she wept. She continued to weep until her weeping took away her sight. Her relations said, "Let us hurry to this woman to reproach her for her excessive weeping." We went to her and said, "O Burayra, what has become of you?"

'She said, "We have become guests residing in a land of exile, waiting to be called and to answer."

'"But this weeping, it has taken away your sight!" we told her.

'"If there be any good in my eyes, then it does not avail them whatever has been taken away from them in this world. If there be any evil, then they should weep longer than this." Then she turned away. Those present said, "Let us leave—for her state, by God, is different from ours."'

Muᶜādha al-ᶜAdawiyya used to say when day broke, 'This is the day I die.' She took no nourishment until evening. At nightfall she would say, 'This is the night I die,' and prayed until morning.[92]

Said Abū Sulaymān al-Dārānī, 'I stayed at the house of Rābiᶜa [al-ᶜAdawiyya] one night. She rose to go to a prayer-niche of hers. I myself went to one side of the house. She stayed up until dawn. At dawn I asked, "What is the reward of the one who gave us the strength to rise this night?"

'She answered, "His reward is that you should observe the fast the next day for Him."'[93]

In her supplication, Shaᶜwāna used to say, 'My Lord, how

[A] The Qur'ān.

intensely I desire to meet Thee, how great my hope for Thy reward! You are the gracious one in whom the hope of the hopeful never fails, in whom the longing of those who long is never thwarted.

'My Lord, if my term is nigh and my deed fails to draw me closer to Thee, then my deficient ways make for acknowledgement of the offence. When You pardon, who is more worthy of that than Thee? When You chastise, who is more just in that than Thee?

'My Lord, I wronged my soul by paying too much attention to it and only Thy comely sight remained for it. Woe to it if Ye should not save it.

'My Lord, You have been charitable to me every day of my life—remove not Thy charity after I die. Verily, I ask of Him who cared for me during my life, in His beneficence, to grant me pardon upon death through His forgiveness.

'My Lord, how can I despair that you will look well upon me after death, when You bring me only the beautiful in my life.

'My Lord, if my sins frighten me so, then my love for Thee gives me sanctuary. Therefore, take charge of what affair of mine befits Thee. Bring Thy favour to someone misled by [her] own ignorance.

'My Lord, if You wanted me to suffer affront, why do You guide me? If You wanted my debasement, then why shield me? So, benefit me with what You guide me in. Enhance for me that with which You shield me.

'My Lord, I do not believe that You will refuse me in a need that I have given my life for.

'My Lord, had I not been tempted by sins, I would not fear Thy punishment. Had I not known Thy nobility, I would not hope for Thy reward.'[94]

Said [Ibrāhīm b. Aḥmad] al-Khawwāṣ, 'We went to Riḥla al-ʿĀbida. She had fasted until she had shrivelled up; wept[95] until she went blind; prayed until she was lame. She prayed sitting down. We greeted her, then reminded her of something about [God's] pardon to ease her affairs. She sighed then said, "My knowledge of my soul has wounded my heart and hurt my liver. My God, I wish God had never created me and that I were nothing." Then she turned to pray.'

If you are among the steadfast (*murābiṭūn*) who are vigilant, self-examining, then it behoves you to study the states of those men and women who are striving, in order to spur your enthusiasm and increase your aspiration. Beware of looking to your contemporaries. Most people on earth you heed lead away from the path of God.

There are countless stories of the those who strive. However, what we have mentioned suffice for illustration. If you desire more, you ought to devote yourself to studying the *Book of the Ornament of God's Friends*,[A] which contains an explanation of the state of the Prophet's Companions, the generation that succeeded them and those after them. Pausing there will make clear to you and your contemporaries your distance from the [original] people of religion.

Your soul may say to you to look to contemporaries. [It may say] that previously the good was prevalent because many upheld it; that if you contradict your contemporaries now, they will consider you insane and mock you; so, agree with them on whatever preoccupies and matters to them, for what applies to them applies to you too. Generalized, calamity becomes tolerable.[B]

Beware of descending by the rope of the soul's deception or being misled by its forgery. Say to your soul, 'Do you see that if a torrential flood drowned the inhabitants in the very places they stood on, unaware of their true situation due to their ignorance; and if you left them and boarded a vessel to save yourself from drowning—would you then consider that the calamity is tolerable because it is generalised? Or would you

[A] *Ḥilyat al-awliyā'* by Abū Nuʿaym.

[B] Meaning that as we are all in the same calamity, we should support each other.

withdraw[96] your approval of them and consider them doltish for their doings and guard against what may befall you?'

But if you forgo their approval for fear of drowning and its torment, which lasts but a moment, how could you fail to flee[97] the eternal torment to which you are exposed at every turn? Would calamity then be tolerable when generalised? The people of Hell-fire are too distracted to discern the general from the specific.

The unbelievers are ruined only by agreeing with the people of their time, who say, *We found our fathers following a religion and we shall follow in their footsteps*.[98]

If you preoccupy yourself with censuring your soul and inducing it to renewed striving, and it renounces its rejection of censure, reproach and rebuke of it, and it learns to see its [earlier] misconception of itself, perhaps then it will be driven[99] away from its oppression.

## CHAPTER SIX

# The Sixth Steadfast Commitment: Self-Reproach and Self-censure

KNOW THAT YOUR WORST ENEMY[1] is your soul inside you. It was created to incite ill and predisposed toward evil and the desertion of the good. You are bidden to purify, reform and lead it through continual subjugation to worship of its Lord and Creator. You must forbid it its passions and wean it from its pleasures. Neglect it and it runs and wanders away, after which you will not [be able to] vanquish it. Reproach, censure and blame it, on the other hand, and it will be the same self-reproaching soul by which God has sworn.[A]

If you aspire to the tranquil soul (*al-nafs al-muṭma'inna*)[2] which is called upon to join the ranks of God's servants, pleasing and content (*rāḍiya marḍiyya*),[3] then do not neglect for one hour to remind and censure it. Do not occupy yourself with admonishing others if you have not firstly admonished yourself.

God's inspiration to Jesus son of Mary (may God grant him peace) was, 'O son of Mary, admonish yourself. When it is admonished,[4] then admonish people. Otherwise, be ashamed of Me.'[5]

God has said, *And remind, for reminding benefits the faithful.*[6]

Your way forward is to attend to your soul and to convince it of its folly and stupidity, and [to ensure] it never draws strength from its cleverness and its own guidance. Associated with fool-

[A] Ghazālī is referring to the Qur'ānic verse LXXV.2: *Nay, I swear by the self-reproaching soul* (al-nafs al-lawwāma).

ishness, it will only grow in haughtiness and pride. Therefore, you should say to it:

Woe unto you, O soul, how great your ignorance is! You claim wisdom, acuity and cleverness, but you are more stupid and foolish than other people.

Do you not know that Paradise and Hellfire are before you, and that you are only a short distance from one of them?[7] Why, then, do you rejoice and mock and amuse yourself so, when you are needed in this weighty matter? You may well abscond today or tomorrow—I see that you think death far, though God thinks it near. Do you not know that everything to come is near and that the distant is what will not come? Do you not know that death comes suddenly without a messenger, and with neither appointment or collusion; that [death] does not come to one thing and leaves another; that it comes in winter as in summer, summer as in winter,[8] day as in night, night as in day, childhood as in youth, youth as in childhood? Indeed, any breath may contain sudden death. If sudden death does not come, then illness will and then lead to death.[9]

Why, O soul, do you not prepare for death, which is nearer to you than anything else? Have you not pondered God's words, *The reckoning of people approaches, but, knowing not, they turn away. No reminder comes to them from their Lord but they listen to it in jest, their hearts amused*?[10]

Woe unto you, O soul, if you are wont to sin against God because you believe He is not looking, then how great your unbelief! If you know that He sees you, how great your insolence and how negligible your shame!

O soul, if a servant of yours, nay, a brother, should confront you with something you dislike, what anger and loathing would you harbour for him? Yet, how recklessly you then expose yourself to God's loathing, anger and stern punishment!

Do you think you can bear His wrath? Far from it! If your cockiness has lulled you away from His painful wrath, then try for yourself! Put yourself under the sun or in the bathhouse for an hour. Bring your fingers close to the flame and find out how you bear up.

Or are you deluded about God's nobility and favour, His disinterestedness with respect to your acts of obedience and worship?

Why do you not rely on His kindness in the weighty matters of your world? When a foe pursues you, why do you devise a stratagem to repel him without relying on God's kindness?

When a need pulls you towards a worldly desire which nothing but gold and silver pieces can fulfil, why do you exhaust yourself in pursuing it and acquiring it with stratagems, instead of relying on God's kindness to lead you to a treasure or to subordinate a servant of His to your need with neither an effort nor a request from you. Do you consider God beneficent in the Hereafter but not in this world?

You should know that there is no substitute for the Way of God (*sunnat Allāh*);[11] that the Lord of this world and the next[12] is One; and *That man shall have only what he strives for.*[13]

Woe unto you, O soul, how amazing are your hypocrisy and pretensions! You lay claim to faith with the tongue while the trace of hypocrisy is evident in you. Has your Lord and Master not said to you, *There is no beast on earth but its sustenance depends on God*?[14] And about the Hereafter, He said, *That man shall have only what he strives for.*[15]

He has specifically taken upon Himself your worldly affairs and spared you pursuit of them. But you deny this through your actions. You rush headlong in pursuit [of the world] in the manner of a spellbound dotard. He has entrusted the matter of the Hereafter to your striving; yet, you shun it in the manner of a fool disdainful.

This is not a sign of faith! If faith were merely verbal (*bi'l-lisān*), why[16] would the hypocrites [be found] at the lowest rung of Hell?

Woe unto you, O soul, it is as if you do not believe in the Day of Reckoning, but think rather that when you die you will be set free and released. Far from it! Do you think that you will be left alone?[17] Were you not a drop of sperm emitted, then a blood clot, then something by design and order? Can He who has the power to do this not quicken the dead?[18]

If this is what you harbour in yourself, then what a denier you are—and how ignorant! You deny that that is from whence He created you—from a drop of sperm He created and cherished you, eased your way, then took back your life and caused you to be buried. Will you deny His word? Yet,[19] He shall resurrect you, if He wills it.[20] If you are not a denier, why are you not on your guard?

If a Jew[A] informed you that the most delectable food may harm you in your illness, you would avoid or abandon it[21] and exert yourself in this. Does the speech of the prophets, who are supported by miracles and the Word of God in the books He has revealed, influence you less than the words of the Jewish [doctor] who counsels you against conjecture, guesswork and supposition [based on] inadequate understanding and knowledge? The wonder is that if a child warned you about a scorpion lodged in your clothing, you would toss away your clothes immediately without asking the child for evidence or proof.

Are the words of the prophets, the learned, the scholars and all the saints lesser for you than the words of a boy, who counts among the unwise? Or are the heat of Hell, its shackles and chains, its infernal tree,[22] pikes, pus, searing sandstorms, vipers and scorpions less significant[23] for you than one scorpion, the pain from which you will feel for a day or less?

These are not the actions of reasonable people. No, if your state were revealed to the beasts they would laugh at you and ridicule your mind.

O soul, if you know all this and believe in it, why delay your action? Death lies in wait for you. It may[24] snatch you without delay.[25] Can you protect yourself from this imminent end?

Suppose you were promised a hundred years' reprieve. Do

[A] That is, a Jewish physician.

you think that he who [only] feeds [his] beast of burden at the lowest point of a steep trail will succeed in completing the route with it? How great your ignorance if you believe this.

What do you think of a man who travels abroad in pursuit of knowledge and lives idly and inactive there for some years, promising himself that he will focus on his studies in his last year before returning to his country? Would you [O soul] not mock his conclusions and his belief that he can gain for himself the knowledge he craves in a short period; or his assumption that discerning persons achieve rank, not through profound study but, solely by relying on God's munificence?

Let us suppose, then, that renewed striving at the end of a lifetime was useful and that it led to higher levels. But perhaps today is your last. Why do you not attend to it? If it occurs to you to delay, then what stymied your impulse and what is your motivation to procrastinate? Is there any other reason besides your inability to oppose your passions because of the pain and trouble of doing so? Do you expect a day when opposition to the passions will not be trying? That day God has simply not created and never will. Paradise is surrounded by nothing but adversities. Those adversities cannot be slight for the souls—that cannot be.

Do you not see how long it has been that you have been promising yourself and saying, 'Tomorrow, tomorrow!'[26] Then, tomorrow indeed arrives and becomes another day. But how do you find it? Do you not know that the morrow that arrives and becomes a day is as good as yesterday? No, today you are more impotent [than yesterday]. And tomorrow you shall be ever more impotent, because passion is like a firmly rooted tree to the eradication of which the servant should be dedicated. If he does not uproot passion because of weakness and procrastinates, he would be like someone who, unable to uproot a tree while still a vigorous youth, procrastinates to another year. However, he knows well that the longer the wait, the stronger the tree, the more firmly planted it will be and the weaker the person who uproots it. Whatever he did not do while young, he certainly will not do in old age.

On the contrary, effort makes old age vigorous, and hardship leads to disciplined alacrity. A young branch accepts to bend, but when dry and old it will not do so.[27]

O dear soul, if you do not understand these clear matters and rely on deferment, why do you claim wisdom? What greater folly is there?

Perhaps you say: 'What prevents me from being upright is my desire for the pleasure of the passions and my impatience with pain and misfortune.' How great your foolishness and shameless your excuse! If you are sincere in this, then seek to luxuriate in passions purified of [their] perennial impurities—though there be no expectation of this except in Paradise.

When you examine your passion, then examine what is opposed to it. So, take the meal that staves off the [other] meals.

What do you say about the intelligence of an ailing person whom a physician has advised to keep away from cold water for three days so he may recuperate and enjoy[28] drinking it the rest of his life?[29] He informs him that if he drank cold water he would fall chronically ill, forbidden to drink it the rest of his life.

So, what must intelligence conclude with respect to passion? Should [the person] bear up for three days for a lifetime of enjoyment? Or should he satisfy his passion now, fearing the pain of three days' contrariety, thereby imposing contrariety for three thousand and three hundred days?[30]

Your whole life is to the blissful eternity that is proper to the denizens of Paradise and the suffering of the denizens of Hell what less than three days are to a lifetime. Would that I knew how the pain of abstaining from the passions could be greater in intensity and length than that of the lowest rungs of Hell! How could someone who cannot withstand the pain of striving bear the painful torment of God?

I see you are fainthearted about how you view your soul thanks either to a latent faithlessness or[31] a clear folly. As to the latent faithlessness, it is but the weakness of your faith in the Day of Reckoning—your lack of knowledge of how great the reward or punishment will be. While clear folly is your reliance on God's nobility and pardon without awareness of His wile,[32] His persuasiveness and His independence of your worship, and your failure to rely on His generosity for a morsel of bread, a grain of property or single word you hear from people. On the contrary, you achieve your goal in this by every stratagem. Because of this ignorance you deserve the title of foolishness from God's Messenger when he said, 'He is astute who adheres to religion and acts for what lies beyond death. He is foolish who follows the appetites of his soul and pleads his longings with God.'[33]

Woe unto you, O soul, you must not let the life of this world gull you nor conceit delude you about God. Watch yourself, for your affairs concern no one else. Do not waste away your moments, for the breaths [of life] are counted. With each breath a part of you departs. Therefore, avail yourself of health before illness; leisure before engagement; wealth before poverty; youthfulness before senility; life before death. And prepare for the Hereafter in accordance with your abiding life in it.

O soul, do you not prepare for winter according to its length and accumulate for it provision, clothing, firewood and other amenities? You do not well depend on God's liberality and kindness to ward off the cold without a coat, wool or firewood, and so on, though He is capable of this.

Do you think the frostiness of Hell less bitter and briefer than the frostiness of winter? Or do you believe the one is not the other and could never be like it? Or that[34] they are related only in intensity and frigidity?

Do you think the servant of God will escape [Hell] without striving?

Far from it! Just as one can only ward off the cold with a coat, fire and other amenities, so the heat of the Fire and its coldness are warded off only through the fortress of God's oneness and the moat of pious deeds.[35] God's kindness is to let you know the method of fortification and to fortune you with its amenities, not to ward off suffering for you without His citadel. Likewise, His kindness is to have created fire for warding off the coldness of winter; He has guided you to the method of drawing it with iron and rock, that you may stave off[36] the winter cold.

Likewise, too, regarding the purchase of firewood and the coat, which your Creator and Master in no wise needs. You buy [the coat] for yourself, for His creations are made for your comfort; and the same for your pious deeds and your striving, He has no need of them. These are your way to salvation. One does good for oneself and commits evil against oneself. God has no need of anyone in this world.

Woe unto you, O soul, shed your ignorance and compare your afterlife with your present world. *Your creation and your resurrection is as one soul*;[37] *As We brought forth the first creation so we shall return it*;[38] you will find no change or alteration in the path of God (*sunnat Allāh*).[39]

Woe unto you, O soul, I see you only acquainting yourself with this world and relishing its company. Separation from [the material world] thus oppresses you as you set about to bring it nearer, confirming your love for it. Even if you are ignorant of God's punishment and reward, the terrors and circumstances of the Resurrection, do you not believe in death which would separate you from the things you love?

Do you think that someone who enters a king's abode [from one end] to exit from the other end, and casts a glance at a comely face—knowing his heart will be enamoured of that face and that he will be forced to part with it—should be counted among the intelligent or[40] among the foolish folk?

Do you not know that this world is the abode of the King of kings?[41] What is it to you but a crossing? After death, nothing in it accompanies those who must traverse it.

This is why the leader of humankind (may God bless him and grant him peace) said, 'The holy spirit has whispered into my heart, "Love whom you will, for ye shall part with him. Do what you will, you are requited for it. Live as you will, for you shall die.'"[42]

Woe unto you, O soul, do you know that he who is attentive to the delights of this world, familiarising himself with it, though death is not far behind, only increases the grief of separation and unwittingly supplies himself with deadly poison?

Do you not see what people long ago built and erected but then they ran their course and vanished, and how God left their enemies to inherit their land and dwellings?

Do you not see[43] that they gathered what they could not eat, build what they could not live in and anticipated what they could not attain?[44] Each one of them[45] had built a castle raised up to the sky, but his abode is a tomb burrowed beneath the soil.

In this world is there greater foolishness and reversal than this? One cultivates his world, certain to depart from it, but when he finally reaches it, his afterlife lies in ruin.

O soul, are you not ashamed to help the foolish in their folly? Even if you do not have the foresight to find your way[46] in these matters, you are predisposed by nature to imitate, to emulate. Therefore, compare the intelligence of the prophets, the learned and the sages with those who are given over to the world. If you yourself believe in intelligence and percipience, then emulate the class that seems more intelligent to you.

O soul, how amazing your dilemma, great your ignorance and manifest your tyranny! Amazing how blind you are to these clear and obvious matters! O soul, perhaps you are intoxicated by the longing for rank, too unsettled either to understand [said matters] or to consider that rank might mean merely the inclination of some people's hearts towards you.

Know that everyone on earth may well bow to you and obey you, but do you not also know that[47] after fifty years neither you nor anyone on earth who adored and bowed to you will remain. There will be a time when you will not be remembered—not a single memory of you. As it is said about the kings who lived before you, *Canst though see anyone of them or hear a whisper from them?*[48]

O soul, how can you sell what endures forever for what cannot last more than fifty years, if it survives even that? This [would be a temptation], if you were an earthly king and both east and west were handed to you, necks were bowed down to you and all matters were in order.[49] How [great] then are your scornful lapse and mischief when all you have been granted is the domain of a shop or a house?

O soul, if—out of your ignorance and sightlessness—you do not renounce this world and long for the next, why then do you not renounce it out of contempt for the meanness of its associates, staying clear of its ample hardships and safeguarding against its swift disappearance?

Why do you not refrain from its trivial things when already its greater things have forsaken you?

Why do you rejoice over a world, even when it favours you, when your country is not devoid of[50] those among the Jews and the Majūs who vie with you over it and who surpass you in comfort and fineries? What a calamity that such trivial [people] should outstrip you!

How great your ignorance, how great your trifle preoccupation! Your opinion fails because you are loathe to place yourself with those near to God among the prophets and the righteous. With proximity to the Lord of the worlds there is everlasting eternity. But you shall rank with those in the footsteps of ignorant fools—for scant days. Pity on you that you should lose both world and faith.

Rush on, O soul, for you are on the verge of ruin! Death approaches you and the warning has come.[A] Who then will pray for you after your passing? Who will fast for you after death? And who will propitiate your Lord?

Woe unto you, O soul, what should matter to you is that your days are numbered? They are your only merchandise. You have traded and lost most of them, and were you to lament for the rest

[A] That is, grey hair.

of your days over your losses, you would leave yourself short. What if you were to lose the remainder, having persisted in your habit?

Do you not know that death is your appointed time? That the grave is your home, dust your blanket and the worm your intimate? The greatest terror lies before you.

O soul, do you not know that the soldiers of death are upon you, waiting for you at the city gate?[51] They are sworn[52] by a solemn oath that they will not leave their positions before they take you with them.

O soul, do you not know that [those who have died] wish to be granted a day's return to this world in order to set aright[53] what has eluded them? They wish to be in your place.[54] If they could, they would buy one day of your life in exchange for the entire world. Meanwhile, you squander your days through negligence and idleness.

Woe unto you, O soul, are you not ashamed? You adorn your exterior for people and contend with God in secret with terrible sins. So, do you feel shame in front of people but not God? Is He less important than those gawking at you?

Do you bid people to be good when you are blemished by vices? Do you summon towards God but flee from Him, remind [others] of God but forget Him?

O soul, do you not know that the guilty are more putrid than excrement? And that excrement cannot be cleaned by excrement? Why then do you desire the purity of others when you yourself are unclean?

Woe unto you, O soul, if you truly understood yourself, you would know that people are afflicted only because of the misfortune of you.[A]

Woe unto you, O soul, you made yourself an ass for Iblīs, who leads you wherever he wills and subjugates you. Despite this, you admire your deeds, even if they are filled with harm.

[A] That is, by the misfortune of having a soul.

How can you admire your deeds in view of the number of your sins and lapses? God cursed Iblīs for a single sin[A] even after he had worshipped Him for two hundred thousand years.[B] Adam was expelled by God from the garden for one sin, although he was His prophet and regent.

Woe unto you, O soul, how deceitful you are! How impudent!

And woe unto you, O soul, how ignorant you are! How bold in sin! Woe to how you believe then violate! How you promise then betray![55]

Woe unto you, O soul, are you bent on building your world with these sins, as if you shall never leave it? Do you not see how the people of the grave once were? They had accumulated much, built high up, harboured hopes far and wide. Yet fallow is their accumulation. Their structures are tombs, their hopes delusions.

Woe unto you, O soul, have you given them any consideration? Have you given a glance? Do you think that they were called to the Hereafter and believe yourself immortal? Far from it, far from it! What you imagine is false. Ever since you came out of your mother's womb your life has been waning. So, build your castle on the face of the earth—[the earth's] bosom shall soon be your grave.[56]

Have you no fear of when the soul will reach the collarbone,[C] when the messengers of your Lord shall come to you in dark colours, gloomy faces and tidings about torment? Would regret benefit you then? Would grief be accepted from you, would you be spared the tears?

[A] Namely, for refusing to bow before Adam.

[B] It is said that before the creation of Adam, Iblīs inhabited the earth, which was called ʿAzāzīl, where he was more diligent and knowledgeable than any angel (cf. Zabīdī 154).

[C] Allusion to Q.lxxv.26. That is, when the soul reaches the collarbone as it exits the body.

O soul, the wonder of all wonders, withal, is that you lay claim to insight and cleverness. In your cleverness you rejoice at the growth of your wealth but grieve not at the diminution of your life. Of what benefit is increased wealth with diminished life?

Woe unto you, O soul, you turn away from the Hereafter but it draws closer to you; you approach the world while it turns away from you.

How many a man faces the day never to finish it? How many a man expects the morrow but never reaches it? You witness this among your brethren, your kin and your neighbours. Observe their distress at death and then you will not return to your folly.

Beware, O hapless soul, a day when He pledges not to spare a servant, to whom He had enjoined [the good] and forbidden [the evil] in this world, the questioning about his deeds—whether important or trifling, overt or covert.

O soul, watch with what body you shall stand before God and with what tongue you shall answer, and be prepared with an answer to the question and for correctness in your answer. In the life that remains before you act during the short days for [the sake of] long days; [act] in the ephemeral abode for the abode of Resurrection; in the abode of sorrow and hardship[57] for that of ease and eternal life. Act before you are no longer [able] to act.

Leave the world by choice, as the free do, before you must leave it by necessity. Rejoice not in what splendours you are fortuned with in this world. Many a man is happy but cheated; many a man is cheated unawares. Woe to the person who will suffer a calamity but is unaware of it, laughing and rejoicing, cheering and frittering away, eating and drinking. In God's book he has earned [the name] 'fuel for the fire'.

O soul, let your gaze upon the world be admonishment, your seeking it out only from necessity, your rejection of [the world] a choice, your pursuit of the Hereafter an anticipation.

Be not of those who are incapable of gratitude for what they receive, who strive to increase what they keep, who forbid other people but not themselves.

O soul, know that religion has no replacement, faith no substitute and the body no other. The person for whom the night and the day are his mount journeys along though he himself moves not.[58]

O soul, take counsel from this admonition—accept this advice. He who shuns the admonition is content with the Fire. And[59] how I find you content with the Fire and oblivious to the admonition! If hardness [of heart] prevents you from accepting admonition, then avail yourself against it by perpetual night vigil and prayer. If it persists, then persevere with the fast.[60] If it persists then, reduce both company and conversation. If it has not ceased, then [resort to goodness] to kin (*ṣilat al-arḥām*) and by kindness to orphans. If it continues further, know that God has sealed and closed your heart, for your heart will have accumulated the darkness of sin in both its interior and exterior.

Therefore, accustom yourself to the Fire. For God has created Paradise and its denizens, and He created Hellfire and its denizens. Each is destined for what he was created for.[61] If you have no more place for admonition, then despair for your soul. [Yet,] despair is one of the most mortal sins,[62] may God keep us from it. When the path of goodness is blocked for you, you may neither despair nor hope.[63]

[In your case], it is delusion, not a hope. But see if you are not overtaken by grief at the misfortune that has befallen you, and whether your eye permits a tear of mercy from you upon your soul.[64] If so, [then know that] the source of tears is the ocean of mercy; and that there remains in you a place for hope. So, persist in your wailing and weeping. Seek aid from the Most Merciful of the merciful; complain to the Kindliest of the kind. Take to seeking aid and do not weary of long complaint [against yourself] and God may yet relieve your weakness and assist you.[65]

For, your misfortune deepens, your calamities worsen, your duration [in affliction] lengthens, your excuses expire and your pleas are withdrawn[66]—in short, no escape or quest, no appeal for help or sanctuary, refuge or haven,[67] save in your Protector—then seek asylum with Him by entreaty. Be humble in your entreaty in proportion to the magnitude of your ignorance and the number of your sins. For He is merciful to the lowly petitioner, aids the eager beseecher and answers the call of the destitute.

Today you come to Him destitute and needful of His mercy, your means are narrow, your path blocked. Your strength is gone and admonitions do not benefit you—no reproach curbs you. Yet, the One asked is generous, the One beseeched is kind, the One appealed to is benevolent and gentle. Mercy is wide, graciousness abundant and pardon complete.

Following the example of Adam your Father, say [O soul], 'O Most Merciful of the merciful, O Compassionate, O Granter of Mercy, O Gentle One, O Great One, O Kind One—I am the inveterate sinner, the reckless one who knows no abstinence, the profligate with no shame.[68] This is the station of the humble petitioner, wretchedly poor and miserably weak, drowning and doomed. Hasten to my succour, give me repose, show me the effects of Your mercy. Let me taste the coolness of Your forgiveness. Bestow upon me the power of Your protection, O Most Merciful of the merciful.'

As Wahb b. Munabbih said, 'When God caused Adam to descend to earth from the Garden,[69] Adam's tears did not cease to flow. So, on the seventh day, while he was grief-stricken, dispirited and embittered, his head bowed, God Exalted apprised him saying, "O Adam, what troubles you so?"[70]

'He said, "Lord, my misfortune is great, my sin envelopes me and I have left the Kingdom of my Lord and come to be in the Abode of Disgrace after [knowing] dignity; in the Abode of Misery after felicity; in the Abode of Hardship after repose; in the Abode of Scourge after health; in the Abode of Transience after constancy; in the Abode of Death and Extinction after eternal life and immortality. How can I not lament my sin?"

'God inspired him, "O Adam, have I not chosen thee for Myself, permitted you My Kingdom, marked you for honour from

Me and warned you about My wrath? Have I not created you with My own hands, blown My spirit into you and made My angels prostrate themselves before you? And yet you disobeyed My command, forgot My pledge and exposed yourself to My wrath?[71] By My Might and Majesty, if the earth were filled with men all like thee, worshipping, exalting, then disobeying Me, I would bring them down to the abodes of the rebellious!" Upon this Adam (peace be upon him) wept for three hundred years.'[72]

ʿUbayd Allāh al-Bajilī used to weep often. While he wept all night he would say, 'Lord, I am one whose sins increase as my life lengthens. I am the one who, resolving to renounce a sinful act, meets yet another impulse. "Woe to you, O ʿUbayd, a sin is not over when its author seeks another. And, woe to you, O ʿUbayd, if the Fire will be your resting place and a shelter. Woe to you, O ʿUbayd, if the striking rods are being prepared for your head. Woe to you, O ʿUbayd, while the requests of seekers are requited,[73] yours may not be."'

Said Manṣūr b. ʿAmmār, 'One night in Kufa I heard a person whispering to his Lord, "Lord, by Your might, I have no wish to disobey or dispute Thee. When I disobeyed Thee, I did so not out of disregard for Thy rank, nor out of objection to Thy punishment, nor out of belittling Thy sight; my soul entices me, my misfortune abetted me in this, and the veil of Thy protection beguiled me. I disobeyed Thee with my ignorance, contradicted Thee with my deeds. Who will rescue me now from Thy torment? Whose rope should I clasp, if Ye should withhold Thy rope from me?

'"O my calamity that I should stand before Thee tomorrow, when the unburdened are told to pass and the overburdened[74] are told to disembark. Shall I pass with the unburdened or disembark with the overburdened?

'"Woe to me! The more I age, the greater my sins. Woe to me! The longer I live, the more numerous my acts of disobedience. How long will I repent,[75] how long will I repeat? Have I not a moment to feel shame before my Lord?"'[76]

These, then, are the ways of the Folk[A] in private prayer (*munājāt*) with their Protector and in the censuring of their souls. Through private prayer they seek reconciliation, while the purpose of their self-censure is instruction and observance. He who neglects self-censure and private prayer has failed himself—he verges on losing God's satisfaction with him.

Thus ends the *Book of Vigilance and Self-Examination* and it is the eighth book of the Quarter of Saving Virtues of the *Revival of the Religious Sciences*. Praise be to God alone, His blessings and peace upon our master Muḥammad and his household.

[A] *Qawm* is translated here as 'Folk', it refers to the Sufis.

# NOTES

## Prologue

[1] Cf. Q. vi.60.
[2] Cf. Q. x.61.
[3] Q. xxi. 47.
[4] Q. xviii.49.
[5] Q. lviii.6.
[6] Q. xcix.6-8.
[7] Q. ii.281.
[8] Q. iii.30.
[9] Q. ii.235.
[10] 'For thy Lord is Ever-Watchful'; or alternatively, 'For thy Lord is a watchtower' Q. lxxxix.14.
[11] A, 5: '*ʿazz man qā'il*'; B, 89: '*ʿazz*'.
[12] Q. iii.200.

## Chapter 1

[1] Q. xci.9-10.
[2] A, 6: '*yuʿāqibahu aw yuʿātibahu*'; B, 90: '*yuʿātibahu aw yuʿāqibahu*'.
[3] A, 6: '*yatanāhī*'; B, 91: '*yuḍāhī*'.
[4] Cf. Q. xxiii.99-100; xxxii.12.
[5] A, 7: '*fa-yaftaḥ*'; B, 91: '*fa-taftaḥ*'.
[6] A, 7: '*wa-yaftaḥ*'; B, 91: '*wa- taftah*'.
[7] A, 7, '*laysa lahu*'; B, 91: '*laysa*'.
[8] A, 7: '*fa-yataḥassar*'; B, 91: '*fa-taḥassar*'.
[9] Makkī, *Qūt* i.108.
[10] Cf. Q. lxxxiii.18.
[11] Q. lxiv.9.
[12] A, 8: '*taqwā*'; B, 92: '*yaqnaʿ*'.
[13] Q. l.18.
[14] A, 8: '*yashruṭ*'; B, 93: '*yashtariṭ*'.
[15] A, 8: '*wa-ṭaʿātihā*'; B, 93: '*ṭaʿātihā*'.
[16] A, 8: '*ʿalā nafsihi*'; B, 93: '*li-nafsihi*'.
[17] Q. li.55.
[18] A, 9: '*muḥāsaba*'; B, 93: '*muḥāsabathu*'.
[19] Q. ii.235.
[20] Q. iv.94.
[21] Q. xlix.6.
[22] Q. l.16.
[23] Ibn al-Mubārak 1101, no. 505.
[24] Ibn Māja, '*al-Zuhd*', ii.1423, no. 4260.
[25] Cf. Zabīdī 94.
[26] Reference unidentified.
[27] A, 10: '*tajiduhā*'; B, 94: '*tajid mā*'.
[28] A, 10: '*baynahumā*'; B, 94: '*baynahunna*'.
[29] *Supra*, Ibn Māja, '*al-Zuhd*', ii.1423, no. 4260.

## Chapter 2

[1] Ibn Māja, '*Muqaddama*', i.24, no. 63-4.
[2] Q. xiii.33.
[3] Q. xcvi.14.
[4] Q. iv.1.
[5] Q. lxx.32-3.

[6] Reference unidentified.
[7] Qushayrī, *Risāla* 150; cf. Sulamī, *Ṭabaqāt* 479-83.
[8] Qushayrī, *Risāla* 51-2.
[9] *Ibid.*, 150.
[10] *Ibid.*
[11] *Ibid.*, 149.
[12] A, 11: '*ṣanam kānā lahā*'; B, 96: '*ṣanam lahā*'.
[13] Zabīdī 96-7.
[14] *Ibid.*, 97.
[15] Reference unidentified.
[16] Qushayrī, *Risāla* 149.
[17] A, 11: '*Mālik b. Dīnār qāla*'; B, 97: '*Mālik b. Dīnār*'.
[18] Reference unidentified.
[19] Cf. Muḥāsibī, *Waṣāyā*, q.v. '*Sharḥ al-murāqaba wa-bayānaha*', 313-5.
[20] A, 11: '*bi-mulāḥaẓa*'; B, 97: '*li-mulāḥaẓa*'.
[21] Qushayrī, *Risāla* 150.
[22] Cf. Zabīdī 97. A, 11: '*ᶜalā al-bāṭin*'; B, 97: '*bil-bāṭin*'.
[23] *Ibid.*, 97.
[24] Reference unidentified.
[25] Q. xcviii.8.
[26] A, 12: '*al-Sanaḥī*'; B, 98: '*al-Sabakhī*'.
[27] Cf. Zabīdī 98.
[28] A, 13: '*ḥāla*'; B, 100: '*ḥāl*'.
[29] A, 13: '*shakk*'; B, 100: '*yashukk*'.
[30] A, 13: '*qad*'; missing in B.
[31] A, 14: '*illā sarīᶜan*'; B, 101: '*sarīᶜan*'.
[32] Zabīdī 101.
[33] A, 14: '*ẓanantuhā*'; B, 101: '*ẓanatu*'.
[34] A, 14: '*annahu qāl*'; B, 101: '*qāl*'.
[35] Reference unidentified.
[36] B, 102: '*fa-qult laᶜallahumā lam yasmaᶜā*'; missing in A.
[37] A, 14: '*marqaᶜatih*'; B, 102: '*raqᶜatih*'.
[38] A, 15: '*wa-lākin*'; B, 102: '*lākin*'.
[39] A, 15: '*kull*'; missing in B, 102.
[40] A, 16: '*li-aḥad ᶜanhu fa-inna fī*'; B, 102: '*ᶜanhu fa-fī*'.
[41] Ibn Ḥanbal iv.24.
[42] A, 16: '*muḥaqqaq*'; B, 103: '*maḥfūẓ*'.
[43] Q. vii.194.
[44] Q. xxix.17.
[45] Q. xxxix.3.
[46] A, 16: '*wa-liyakun*'; B, 103: '*wa-liljawāb*'.
[47] A, 16: '*fattih*'; B, 103: '*futāt*'.
[48] Makkī, *Qūt* ii.162.
[49] Zabīdī 103.
[50] *Ibid.*
[51] A, 17: '*yaḥibbuh*'; B, 104: '*yaḥibb*'.
[52] Q. xviii.104.
[53] Abū Nuᶜaym, *Ḥilya*, vi.199.
[54] Ḥadīth unidentified.
[55] B, 105: '*wa-tarakūhā*'; missing in A.
[56] Ibn Māja, '*Fitna*', ii.1330-31, no. 4014.
[57] Q. xvii.36.
[58] Bukhārī, '*Waṣāyā*', iv.50, no. 11; Muslim '*al-Birr*', iv.290, no. 2563.
[59] Ibn Ḥanbal ii.173.
[60] Q. iv.113.
[61] Q. xvi.43.
[62] Q. xcii.12.
[63] Q. lxxv.19.
[64] Q. xvi.9.
[65] Cf. Zabīdī 107.
[66] Cf. Zabīdī 107.

[67] *Ibid.*

[68] A, 20: '*al-ishtighāl bil-tafakkur*'; B, 107: '*al-ishtighāl bil-tafkīr*'.

[69] Q. LXV.1.

[70] Q. XXVIII.77.

[71] A, 21: '*al-ḥāla*'; B, 108: '*al-ḥāl*'.

[72] Ibn Ḥanbal VI.446.

[73] Cf. Zabīdī 109.

[74] A, 22: '*al-tabaṣṣur*'; B, 109: '*al-tabṣira*'.

[75] A, 22: '*al-shahwāt*'; B, 109: '*al-shahwa*'.

[76] A, 22: '*qawm*'; B, 109: '*qism*'.

[77] A, 22: '*al-fikr*'; B, 109: '*al-fikra*'.

[78] A, 22: '*ṣanʿ*'; B, 109: '*min ṣanʿ*'.

[79] Ibn Ḥanbal V.299, 311.

## Chapter 3

[1] Q. LIX.17.

[2] Cf. Zabīdī 109.

[3] *Ibid.*

[4] Q. XXIV.31.

[5] Ibn Ḥanbal II.21.

[6] Q. VII.201.

[7] A, 23: '*mimmā*'; B, 112: '*ammā*'. Mālik, *Muwaṭṭa'*, I.98.

[8] A, 24: '*min*'; B, 112: '*lā min*'.

[9] A, 24: '*ḥattā dakhal*'; B, 112: '*fa-dakhal*'.

[10] Q. LXXV.2.

[11] As one bridles the camel. A, 24: '*dhammahā*'; B, 113: '*zammahā*'.

[12] Cf. Zabīdī 113.

[13] A, 24: '*raḥam Allāh*'; missing in B, 113.

[14] A, 24: '*raḥam Allāh*'; missing in B, 113.

[15] A, 24: '*ḥattā*'; B, 113: '*imra' imra' ḥattā*'.

[16] Cf. Zabīdī 113.

[17] A, 26: '*yawman*'; B, 114: '*yawman ʿumrahu*'.

[18] A, 26 and B, 114 say 1,021, but 1,521 is meant.

[19] Cf. Zabīdī 114.

[20] A, 26: '*maʿṣiya*'; B, 114: '*kull maʿṣiya*'.

[21] Q. LVIII.6.

## Chapter 4

[1] A, 26: '*halākihā*'; B, 115: '*halākihā*'.

[2] A, 26: '*yanbaghī*'; B, 115: '*fa-yanbaghī*'.

[3] A, 27: '*yabisat*'; B, 115: '*fashshat*'.

[4] A, 27: '*fī*'; B, 115: '*min*'.

[5] A, 27: '*al-Karībī*'; B, 115: '*al-Kartanī*'.

[6] A, 27: '*fa-aḥtajtu*'; B, 116: '*fa-aḥtajtu*'.

[7] A, 27: '*aʿnī*'; B, 116: '*uʿayyin*'.

[8] A, 27: '*fa-yajib lahu*'; B, 116: '*fa-yajib*'.

[9] A, 27: '*baqarat*'; B, 116: '*nafarat*'.

[10] Cf. Zabīdī 116.

[11] A, 17: '*a-nawm*'; B, 116: '*nawm*'.

[12] A, 27: '*yuʿātib*'; B, 116: '*yuʿāqib*'.

[13] Abū Nuʿaym *Ḥilya* VI.182.

[14] A, 28: 'ʿ*an*'; B, 117: 'ʿ*an*'.

[15] A, 28: '*yā fulān idʿī liya yā fulān idʿī liya*'; B, 117: '*yā fulān idʿī liya*'.

[16] A, 28: '*ijʿal al-janna ma'ābahum*'; B, 117: '*ijʿal ma'ābahum al-janna*'.

[17] Cf. Zabīdī 117.

[18] *Ibid.*

[19] A, 28: '*ḥājatahu*'; B, 118: '*ḥāja*'.

[20] Cf. Zabīdī 118.

[21] A, 29: '*baṭā'ir fī hā'iṭihi*'; B, 118: '*fī ḥā'iṭihi*'.

[22] Cf. Zabīdī 118-19.

[23] *Ibid.*, 119.

## Chapter 5

[1] *Ibid.*, 120.
[2] Q. xxiii.60.
[3] Zabīdī 120.
[4] *Ibid.*, 121.
[5] *Ibid.*, 121.
[6] A, 31: '*aʿyunihim*'; B, 121: "ʿaynihim'.
[7] Cf. Makkī, *Qūt* i.32, 265.
[8] Zabīdī 121.
[9] Qushayrī, *Risāla* 21.
[10] A, 32: '*yakrahūn*'; B, 122: '*yakrahūn min*'.
[11] Cf. Abū Dā'ūd, *Sunan* '*K. al-adab*', iv.360, no. 5236; and Ibn Māja, *Sunan*, '*K. al-zuhd*', ii.1393, no. 4160.
[12] Cf. Zabīdī 123.
[13] *Ibid.*
[14] A, 32: '*fa-qāl*'; B, 123: '*fa-yaqūl*'.
[15] A, 32: '*ḥabbabat*'; B, 124: '*ḥabbab*'.
[16] Cf. Zabīdī 124.
[17] Qushayrī, *Risāla* 17.
[18] A, 32: '*ḥuẓūẓihim*'; B, 124: '*ḥuẓwa*'.
[19] A, 33: '*qāl lahu*'; B, 124: '*qāl*'.
[20] A, 34: "ʿ*an*'; B, 125: '*idh*'.
[21] Abū Nuʿaym, *Ḥilya* x.5.
[22] Cf, Zabīdī 126.
[23] *Ibid.*
[24] Cf. Abū Nuʿaym, *Ḥilya* vi.229.
[25] Cf. Zabīdī 126.
[26] *Ibid.*, 127.
[27] *Ibid.*, 126.
[28] *Ibid.*, 127.
[29] *Ibid.*, 127.
[30] A, 34: '*Ḥārith*'; B, 127: '*Ḥarth*'.
[31] A, 35: '*arā*'; B, 127: '*arqā*'.
[32] Cf. Zabīdī 128.
[33] A, 35: '*fī kull*'; B, 128: '*kull*'.
[34] A, 35: '*kull*'; B, 128: '*fī kull*'.
[35] Q. cxii.1.
[36] Cf. Abū Nuʿaym, *Ḥilya* v.40.
[37] *Ibid.*, iii.166.
[38] *Ibid.*, ii.88-9.
[39] A, 36: '*yamūd*'; B, 130: '*tamīd*'.
[40] Cf. Zabīdī 130.
[41] *Ibid.*, 130.
[42] A, 36: '*la-nuzāḥimahum ʿalayhi ziḥāman*'; B, 130: '*la-nuzāḥimannahum ziḥāman*'.
[43] Cf. Zabīdī 130.
[44] Q. lii.27.
[45] Cf. Zabīdī 131.
[46] *Ibid.*, 131.
[47] *Ibid.*, 132.
[48] *Ibid.*, 132.
[49] *Ibid.*, 132.
[50] Abū Nuʿaym, *Ḥilya* vi.234.
[51] A, 38: '*ṭawā'if*'; B, 133: '*ṭarā'if*'.
[52] A, 38: '*anā bi-rawḍa*'; B, 133: *bi-rawḍa*'.
[53] A, 38: '*wa-idhā*'; B, 133: '*fa-idhā*'.
[54] Q. iii.30.
[55] A, 38: '*kharra*'; B, 133: '*kharra maʿahā*'.
[56] A, 38: '*fa-qāl*'; B, 133: '*wa-qāl*'.
[57] A, 38: '*thumma qāl*'; B, 134: '*thumma rajaʿ*'.
[58] Q. xxxix.47.
[59] A, 39: '*min faḍlika*'; B, 134: '*bi-faḍlika*'.
[60] Q. iii.185.
[61] A, 39: '*fī-mā*'; B, 134: '*mimmā*'.
[62] A, 39: '*mi'dhar*'; B, 134: '*mi'zar*'.
[63] A, 39: '*dhull*'; B, 134: '*dhilla*'.
[64] A, 39: '*bi-Qimma*'; B, 134:

*'bi-Qunna'*. Qunna is a valley in Mesopotamia.

65 A, 40: *'yaẓhar'*; B, 135: *'yaẓfar'*.

66 Cf. Zabīdī 135.

67 *Ibid.*, 135.

68 A, 40: *'kam'*; B, 135: *'fa-kam'*.

69 Abū Nuʿaym, *Ḥilya* v.79.

70 A, 40: *'ṣallat al-ʿatma qāmat'*; B, 138: *'ṣallat qāmat'*.

71 A, 41: *'wa-ʿizzatuka li-hādhā da'bī wa-da'bika mā ābqaytanī wa-ʿizzatuhā law antahartanī'*; B, 138: *'wa-ʿizzatuka law antahartanī'*.

72 A, 41: *'ʿan'*; B, 138: *'min'*.

73 Cf. Zabīdī 138.

74 *Ibid.*, 138.

75 *'Wa annī liya bil-biqā''* is repeated in A, 41, but not in B, 138. See Zabīdī 138.

76 A, 41: *'ahl al-Ayka'*; B, 138: *'ahl al-abilla'*. Abilla is a place near Basra, probably where descendants of the famed African slave-soldiers had settled.

77 Cf. Zabīdī 139.

78 A, 41: *'fa-iltamastuhā'*; B, 139: *'fa-lamastuhā'*.

79 Cf. Zabīdī 139.

80 The correct name is Abū Hishām (Zabīdī 139).

81 A, 42: *'taqūl'*; B, 139: *'wa-taqūl'*.

82 A, 42: *'atarāhā'*; B, 139: *'tarāhā'*.

83 Q. XXXIX.47.

84 A, 42: *'fa-qultu'*; B, 139: *'qultu'*.

85 A, 42: *'qad waqaʿ'*; B, 139: *'waqaʿ'*.

86 A, 42: *'ʿUfayra'*; B, 140: *'Ghufayra'*.

87 A, 42: *'fa-qulnā lahā'*; B, 140: *'fa-qulnā'*.

88 A, 42: *'ʿUfayra'*; B, 140: *'Ghufayra'*.

89 Abū Nuʿaym, *Ḥilya* x.227, which contains a similar story.

90 A, 43: *'wa dhahabtu fī baʿḍ ḥawā'ijī wa-qultu: lā tabraḥi ḥattā anṣarif ilayki qāla fa-inṣaraftu fa-lam ajidhā fī al-mawḍiʿ'*; B, 140: *'fa-inṣaraftu fa-lam ajidhā fa-inṣaraftuhā'*.

91 Cf. Zabīdī 140.

92 Cf. Zabīdī 141.

93 *Ibid.*, 141.

94 *Ibid.*, 142.

95 A, 44: *'bakit'*; B, 142: *'bakiyat'*.

96 A, 44. *'tatrukīna'*; B, 147: *'tatrukī'*.

97 A, 45: *'tahrabīna'*; B, 147: *'tahrabī'*.

98 Q. XLIII.23.

99 A, 45: *'tanzajir'*; B, 147: *'li-tanzajir'*.

## Chapter 6

1 A,45: *'ʿaduwwuka'*; B, 148; *'ʿaduww laka'*.

2 Cf. Q. LXXXIX.27.

3 Cf. Q. LXXXIX.28.

4 A, 45: *'ittaʿaẓuka'*; B, 148: *'ittaʿaẓtu'*.

5 Cf. Zabīdī 148.

6 Q. LI.55.

7 A, 45: *'wa-annaki'*; B, 148: *'wa-anti'*.

8 A, 46: *'wa-lā ya'tī fī shay' dūn shay' wa-lā fī shitā' dūn ṣayf'*; *'lā ya'tī fī shitā' dūn ṣayf wa-lā fī ṣayf dūn shitā''*.

9 Cf. Zabīdī 148.

10 Q. XXI.1-3.

11 Cf. Q.XXXIII.62.

12 A, 47: *'al-ākhira wa'l-dunyā'*; B,

149: '*al-dunyā wa'l-ākhira*'.

[13] Q. LIII.39.

[14] Q. XI.6.

[15] Q. LIII.39.

[16] A, 47: '*fa-limā*'; B, 149: '*fa-limā dhā*'.

[17] Cf. Q.LXXV.36.

[18] Cf. Q. LXXV.36-40.

[19] A, 47: '*thumma idhā*'; B, 150: '*idhā*'.

[20] Cf. Q.LXXX.22.

[21] A, 47: '*taraktuhu*'; B, 150: '*taraktīhi*'.

[22] Cf. Q. XXXVII.62; XLIV.43; LVI.52.

[23] A, 47: '*aḥqar*'; B, 150: '*aqṣar*'.

[24] A, 47: '*li-ʿallahu*'; B, 150: '*li-allaki*'.

[25] A, 47: '*muhla*'; B, 150: '*mahl*'.

[26] A, 48: '*mundh*'; B, 150: '*mudh*'.

[27] A, 48: '*yaqbal*'; B, 151: '*yanfa' fīh*'.

[28] A, 48: '*yahna*'; B, 151: '*yatahanna*'.

[29] A, 48, '*ʿumrihi*'; B, 151: '*al-ʿumr*'.

[30] A, 48: '*fa-mā muqtaḍā al-ʿaql fī qaḍā ḥaqq al-shahwa ayaṣbir thalāthat ayyām li-yatanaʿʿam ṭūl al-ʿumr am yaqḍī shahwatahu fī al-ḥāl khawfan min alam al-mukhālafa thalāthat ayyām ḥattā yalzamhu alam al-mukhālafa thulth mi'a yawm wa-thalāthat alf yawm*'; B, 151: '*yaqḍī shahwatahu fī al-ḥāl khawfan min alam al-mukhālafa thalāthat ayyām li-yatanaʿʿam ṭūl al-ʿumr*'.

[31] A, 49: '*li-nafsihi illā*'; B, 151: '*ilā nafsihi ammā*'.

[32] A, 49: '*makrihi*'; B, 151: '*mukararihi*'.

[33] Cf. Zabīdī 151. A, 49: '*al-amāniyy*'; missing in B, 151.

[34] A, 49: '*aw an*'; B, 152: '*wa-an*'.

[35] Cf. Zabīdī 152.

[36] A, 49: '*tadfaʿī*'; B, 152: '*tadfaʿ*'.

[37] Q.XXXI.28.

[38] Q.XXI.104.

[39] Cf. Q.XXXV.43.

[40] A, 50: '*am*'; B, 152: '*aw*'.

[41] A, 50: '*li-malik al-mulūk*'; B, 152: '*malik min al-mulūk*'.

[42] Zabīdī 152.

[43] A, 50: '*tarīnahum*'; B, 152: '*tarāhum*'.

[44] Cf. Zabīdī 153.

[45] A, 50: '*wāḥid*'; B, 153: '*wāḥid minhum*'.

[46] A, 50: '*tahtadī*'; B, 153: '*tahtadīn*'.

[47] A, 51: '*afa-mā taʿrifīn annahu*'; B, 153: '*amā taʿrifīn anna*'.

[48] Q. XIX.98.

[49] A, 51: '*asbāb*'; B, 152: '*al-asmā'*'.

[50] A, 51: '*takhlū*'; B, 153: '*yakhlū*'.

[51] Cf. Zabīdī 154.

[52] A, 52: '*ʿalā anfusihim kulluhum*'; B, 154: '*kulluhum ʿalā anfusihim*'.

[53] A, 52: '*li-yashtaghilū*'; B, 154: '*yashtaghilūn*'.

[54] Zabīdī 154.

[55] A, 52: '*kam taʿhadīna fa-taghdarīn*'; B, 154: '*kam taʿhadīna maʿa Allāh fa-taghdadirīn*'.

[56] Cf. Zabīdī 155.

[57] A, 53: '*naṣīb*'; B, 155: '*naṣb*'.

[58] Cf. Zabīdī 155.

[59] A, 53: '*fa-in*'; B, 156: '*wa-in*'.

[60] A, 53: '*fa-bil-muwāẓaba ʿalā al-ṣiyām*'; B, 156: '*fal-muwāẓaba ʿalā al-ṣiyām fa-inna jawʿ yasudd majārī al-*

*shayṭān fī al-ʿurūq*'.

[61] Makkī, *Qūt* II.160.

[62] A, 54: '*kabīra*'; B, B, 156; '*min raḥmat Allāh taʿālā kabīra*'.

[63] A, 54: '*al-khayr ʿalayki*'; B, 156; '*al-khayr*'.

[64] Zabīdī 156.

[65] A, 54: '*yughīthuki*'; B, 156: '*yuʿīnuki*'.

[66] A, 54: '*rāḥat*'; B, 156: '*inzāḥat*'.

[67] A, 54: '*lā malja' wa-lā manja'*'; B, 156: '*lā manja' wa-lā malja'*'.

[68] A, 54: '*astaḥy*'; B, 156: '*yastaḥy*'.

[69] A, 54: '*min al-janna ilā al-arḍ*'; B, 157: '*ilā al-arḍ min al-janna*'.

[70] A, 54: '*arā*'; B, 157: '*addā*'.

[71] A, 55: '*li-sakhaṭī*'; B, 157: '*li-sulṭī*'.

[72] Zabīdī 157.

[73] A, 55: '*ḥawā'ij*'; B, 158; '*ḥāja*'.

[74] A, 55: '*qīla lil-muthaqqalīn*'; B, 158: '*lil-muthaqqalīn*'.

[75] A, 55; '*fa-ilā matā*'; B, 158; '*qāla matā*'.

[76] Abū Nuʿaym, *Ḥilya* IX.328.

# APPENDIX

## PERSONS CITED IN TEXT — EXCLUDING PROPHETS

ʿABD ALLĀH B. DĀʾŪD, ABŪ ʿABD AL-RAḤMĀN [d. 213/828]. Traditionist and ascetic from Basra. [Samʿānī II.354; Dhahabī (2) I.337-38, no. 320]

ʿABD ALLĀH B. DĪNĀR AL-ʿADAWĪ [d. 127/744]. Client of the Companion ʿAbd Allāh b. ʿUmar (d. 73/693-4).

ʿABD ALLĀH B. AL-ḤASAN B. AL-ḤASAN B. ʿALĪ B. ABĪ ṬĀLIB [d. 145/762-3]. Claimed the leadership of the ʿAlīds, or followers of ʿAlī b. Abī Ṭālib, and put his son Muḥammad forward as the Mahdī.

ʿABD ALLĀH IBN SALĀM [d. 43/663]. Hailing from the Banū Qaynuqāʿ tribe, he was one of the first learned Jews in Medina to convert to Islam after the Prophet's arrival there. When Ibn Salām embraced Islam, the Prophet then gave him the name ʿAbd Allāh. Even before his conversion, which other sources date to when the Prophet was still in Mecca, he claimed that Muḥammad was mentioned in the Torah. In Medina, he assisted the Prophet in his dialogue with the Jewish tribes and insisted that Muslims apply the Jewish ritual killing by stoning for adulterers and like. He is also known to have extolled the Caliph ʿUthmān profusely and deeply lamented his passing. [J. H. A. Juynboll, 303-4, 324; Madelung, 395; *EI*[2]]

ʿABD ALLĀH B. QAYS, *see* Abū Mūsā ʿAbd Allāh b. Qays al-Ashʿarī.

ʿABD ALLĀH B. ʿUMAR B. AL-KHAṬṬĀB [d. 73/693]. Still young when the Prophet was alive, ʿAbd Allāh nevertheless transmitted a large number of traditions from the Prophet. He remained aloof of political intrigues, although he is known to have rebuked al-Ḥajjāj b. Yūsuf (d. 714), governor and Caliph ʿAbd al-Malik's lieutenant, before a large crowd. His moral strength earned him a reputation for fearlessness. [Abū Nuʿaym I.292-314; Azmi 45]

ʿABD AL-WĀḤID B. ZAYD AL-BAṢRĪ [d. 177/193]. Ascetic from Basra known especially for his edifying preaching. [Abū Nuʿaym VI.155-65; Ibn al-Jawzī III.240-44; Massignon, *Essai*, 213-215]

ABŪ ʿABD ALLĀH MUḤAMMAD B. KHAFĪFA AL-SHIRĀZĪ [d. 371/

981-82]. Famous mystic from Shirāz. Associated with Jarayrī, Ibn ʿAṭāʾ and Ruwaym among others. He professed the Ẓāhirite doctrine of legal interpretation, though theologically he was an Ashʿarite. He also protected the persecuted followers of Ḥallāj. [Sulamī 462-66; Abū Nuʿaym x.385-387; Samʿānī III.492; Ibn Mulaqqin 290-294; Jāmī II.235-36; *EI*² III.846-47]

ABŪ BAKR B. ʿAYYĀSH B. SĀLIM AL-ASADĪ AL-KŪFĪ [d. 193/809]. Learned man from Kufa reputed for his knowledge of the Qurʾān. [Dhahabī (2) I.265-66, no. 852; Zabīdī 128]

ABŪ BAKR MUḤAMMAD B. ʿALĪ B. JAʿFAR AL-KATTĀNĪ [d. 322/933-34]. Hailed from Baghdad, where he was a member of the Sufi circles of Junayd, Kharrāz and Nūrī, and travelled to Mecca, where he died. He used to say, 'Be in this world with your body but in the next with your heart.' [Qushayrī 45; Sulamī 373-77; Abū Nuʿaym x.357-58]

ABŪ BAKR AL-ṢIDDĪQ [d. 13/634]. A close, early Companion of the Prophet and first caliph (*r.* 11/632-13/634). From Mecca he fled with the Prophet to Medina, where he continued as a major pillar of the nascent Muslim community. Sufis tend to associate him with the contemplative life. [Ibn Ḥanbal, *K. al-zuhd* 13-9; Nabhānī I.127-28; Hujwīrī 97-9; *EI*² I.109-11]

ABŪ DARDĀʾ ʿUWAYMIR B. ZAYD AL-KHAZRAJĪ [d. 32/652]. A highly respected legal authority whom ʿUmar once sent out as a teacher with Ibn Masʿūd to both Kufa and Damascus. As an ascetic he advocated meditation and privileged the fear of God to mechanical ritual. He taught that one obtained nothing from God before renouncing the world. Died in Damascus. [Ibn Ḥanbal 55-65; Massignon 158]

ABŪ DHARR B. JUNDAB AL-GHIFĀRĪ [d. 32 or 33/652-654]. One of the first to embrace Islam, Abū Dharr transmitted many traditions incorporated in the collections of Bukhārī and Muslim, many of them on poverty. To later generations he stood as the prototype of the *faqīr*. [Ibn Ḥanbal 77-9; Abū Nuʿaym I.156; Massignon 158-9; Schimmel 28; *EI*² I.118]

ABŪ ḤAFṢ ʿAMR B. MASLAMA AL-ḤADDĀD [d. *ca.* 260/873]. Lived in a town next to Nīshāpūr. He taught that external propriety reflected internal propriety. [Qushayrī 28]

ABŪ AL-ḤASAN KAHMAS B. AL-ḤASAN AL-TAMĪMĪ AL-BAṢRĪ [d. 149/766]. A transmitter of traditions. [Zabīdī 127]

ABŪ HĀSHIM AL-QURASHĪ. A Qurayshī of Banī ʿĀmir. [Zabīdī 139]

ABŪ MUḤAMMAD AḤMAD B. MUḤAMMAD AL-JARAYRĪ [d. 311/

923-4]. A *mutakallim* and one of the best-known companions of Junayd. He taught that nothing was weightier than practice and that domination by the self left one captive to the passions. Everything, he said, had its right with God but nothing had greater right than wisdom. [Qushayrī 39-40; Sulamī 259-64; *Tarīkh Baghdād* IV.430-34]

ABŪ MUḤAMMAD AL-MUGHĀZILĪ. Possibly Abū Jaʿfar Muḥammad b. Manṣūr al-Mughāzilī (d. 254/868), a traditionist. [Ibn Ḥajar (2) II.136-37, no. 6345; Zabīdī 124]

ABŪ MŪSĀ ʿABD ALLĀH B. QAYS AL-ASHʿARĪ [d. 42/622 or 52/672]. *Amīr* (governor) of Basra and then of Kufa. He was named arbiter in the conflict that pitted ʿAlī against Muʿāwiya at Ṣiffīn. Also known for his successful military campaign in Iraq. [Zabīdī 47; *EI*² I.716-17; cf. Ibn Ḥajar (1) II.359-60]

ABŪ MUSLIM ʿABD ALLĀH B. THAWBAT AL-KHAWLĀNĪ [d. 62/682]. Of Yemenite origin, he was one of eight members of the succeeding generation, or the *Tābiʿūn*, recognised for their asceticism. He was warmly received by Abū Bakr and ʿUmar and later travelled to Syria. [Abū Nuʿaym II.122-31, V.120-22; Ibn al-Jawzī IV.180-86; *EI*² IV.1167]

ABŪ NUʿAYM AḤMAD AL-IṢBĀHĀNĪ [d. 430/1038]. Author of an invaluable Sufi biographical collection, *Ḥilyat al-awliyā'*. It is said that after he was banished from a mosque where he used to preach, the mosque collapsed, crushing some of his opponents to death. Upon his return, other opponents turned against him again and soon found their untimely end. [Nabhābī I.486-87]

ABŪ SULAYMĀN ʿABD AL-RAHMĀN B. ʿAṬIYYAH AL-DĀRĀNĪ [d. 205/820]. Though hailing from Wāsiṭ, Abū Sulaymān was an early influential exponent of Sufism in Syria. He later travelled to Dārayā (on the outskirts of Damascus), from which his name is derived. He is mentioned as having accepted *ḥadīths* from the celebrated traditionist and ascetic Sufyān al-Thawrī. Abū Sulaymān taught Ibn Abī al-Ḥawārī, with whom he consolidated Baṣran Sufism in Syria. In Baṣra, Mālik b. Dīnār had been the first to regularize Sufi teachings, but it was largely with ʿUbayda ʿAbd al-Wāḥid b. Zayd (d. 177/793), Abū Sulaymān al-Dārānī's teacher, that Sufism had taken root in that region. [Sulamī 76; Qushayrī 25; Ibn al-Mulaqqin 386-97; Jāmī 39-40, 65; Nabhānī II.144; Hujwīrī 143-44; Dhahabī I.203-07; Massignon, *Essai* 219]

ABŪ TALḤA AL-ANṢĀRĪ AL-KHAZRAJĪ, ZAYD B. SAHL [d. 34/654]. A Companion of the Prophet. His wife was Umm Sulaym bint Milḥam, mother of Anas b. Mālik, who reported that in order to marry her Abū Talḥa had agreed to embrace Islam. He fought at the Battles of Uḥūd and Ḥunayn and died at seventy years old in Medina. [Ibn Saʿd v.53-4]

ABŪ ʿUTHMĀN AL-MAGHRIBĪ [d. 373/983-84]. Hailed from Qayrawān and associated with Abū ʿAlī b. al-Kātib, Abū ʿAmr and al-Zajjājī, Abū al-Ḥasan b. al-Ṣā'iʿ al-Dīnawarī and other learned men. Biographers describe him as exhibiting rigour, discipline and abstinence. Died in Nīshāpūr. [Qushayrī 50; Sulamī 479-83]

ABŪ ʿUTHMĀN SAʿĪD B. ISMĀʿĪL AL-NISĀBŪRĪ [d. 298/910-11]. A mystic from Rayy, Abū ʿUthmān was a disciple of Yaḥyā b. Muʿādh Rāzī and Shāh Kirmānī. He maintained relations with Baghdad's Sufis, notably Junayd and Ruwaym. In Nīshāpūr, he married the daughter of Abū Ḥafṣ and became the third master of the Malāmatiyya there, after Abū Ḥafṣ and Hamdūn. Unlike other Malāmatiyya, he composed some works. [Qushayrī 19; Samʿānī II.298-99; Ibn Khallikān II. 369-70; Bauer 62; cf. Hujwīrī 132-34 (Nicholson)]

AL-AḤNAF B. QAYS AL-ʿANBAR AL-BAṢRĪ AL-TAMĪMĪ [d. 67/686-7]. A second generation Muslim and the first from the Tamīm tribe to embrace Islam. He took part in important military campaigns in Iran. He did not fight in the Battle of the Camel but took part in the Battle of Ṣiffīn. He was noted for his aphorisms and died in Kufa at seventy years old. [Ibn Khallikān I.635-44; *EI*$^2$ I.304]

ʿĀ'ISHA [d. 57/676]. Daughter of Abū Bakr and wife of the Prophet. She transmitted many important utterances by the Prophet and was known for her poetic proclivities. [Abū Nuʿaym I.43-50; Ibn al-Jawzī II.6-19; Ibn Ḥajar (I) IV.359-61, no. 704; *EI*$^2$ I.317-18]

ʿALĪ B. ABĪ ṬĀLIB [d. 40/661]. A cousin and son-in-law of the Prophet. He accepted reluctantly to be the fourth caliph after ʿUthmān's assassination (and was later named *Imām* by Shīʿa Muslims). Sufis revere him for his breadth of knowledge, piety and ascetic mien. Died at Kufa by a poisoned arrow. [Ibn Ḥanbal, *K. al-zuhd* 47-52; Hujwīrī 101-02; *EI*$^2$ II.381-86]

ʿĀMIR B. ʿABD ALLĀH B. ʿABD QAYS AL-ʿANBARĪ AL-BAṢRĪ [d. 60/679). A *Tābiʿī*, known as ʿĀmir b. ʿAbd Qays and reputed for his austerity and unusual deeds. Nabhānī mentions one such deed he performed with a lion presumably during his travel to Syria. [Abū Nuʿaym II.87-95; Bukhārī *Tarīkh* VI.447; Nabhānī II.136-7; *EI*$^2$ I.453; Zabīdī 129]

ANAS B. MĀLIK [d. 91-3/709-11]. Anas was a young boy when the Prophet came to Medina. He transmitted a large number of traditions to his many students, who used them for their own collections. His transmissions are recorded by Bukhārī and Muslim. On the issue of written traditions, however, he insisted that '[we] do not value the knowledge of those who have not written down.' He took part in several military expeditions. [Nabhānī I.130; Ibn ʿAbd al-Barr, *Istīʿāb* no. 277; Azmi 49; *EI²* I.482]

AL-ASWAD B. YAZĪD QAYS AL-NAKHAʿĪ, ABŪ ʿUMAR [d. 80/699-700]. An ascetic known for his devotion to the pilgrimage, which he is said to have performed eighty times, and for his constant night vigils. [Abū Nuʿaym II.102-5]

ʿAṬĀ' AL-SULAMĪ [d. 121/738-9]. Mystic from Basra. [Abū Nuʿaym VI.215-27]

BISHR B. AL-ḤĀRITH AL-ḤĀFĪ [d. 226 or 227/841-42]. A companion of al-Fuḍayl b. ʿIyāḍ, Bishr 'the Barefooted' (because he considered even shoes 'a veil from God'). He hailed from Marw and lived in Baghdad. He was knowledgeable in the religious sciences, and taught that whoever wished to be honoured in this world and praised in the next must forgo three things: asking from others, vilifying others and accepting an invitation for a meal—since God alone, not the host, is the benefactor. [Abū Nuʿaym VIII, 336; Sulamī 39-47; Ibn al-Jawzī II.183-90; Ibn Khallikān I.274-77; Jāmī 48-9; Nabhānī I.607-08; Hujwīrī 135-6; Zabīdī 127; Schimmel 37-8; *EI²* I.1282-84]

DĀ'ŪD B. NUṢAYR AL-ṬĀ'Ī, ABŪ SULAYMĀN [d. 160/776-77 or 162/778-79]. A Kufan contemporary of Ibrāhīm b. Adham and a pupil of Abū Ḥanīfa in jurisprudence and Ḥabīb Rāʿī in early 'Sufism'. However, he shunned the authority of certain professional scholars. Although learned from them, he preferred silence. He reputedly either buried his books or threw them into the Euphrates. His brand of asceticism was coloured by grief and seclusion. [Abū Nuʿaym VII.335-66; Hujwīrī 140-1; Ibn al-Jawzī III.74-82; Ibn Khallikān II.259-63; ʿAṭṭār 138-42; Nabhānī, *Karāmāt al-awliyā'* II.63-4; Azmi 126]

DHŪ AL-NŪN AL-MIṢRĪ [d. 245/860]. Born at Ekhmim in Upper Egypt. He was renowned for his alchemist and mystical predilections, and was thought to understand Egyptian hieroglyphs. At one time, he was arrested on charges of heresy but was soon released. [Abū Nuʿaym IX.331-95; Sulamī 15-26; Ibn al-Jawzī IV.287-93; Ibn Khallikān I.315-18; Massignon, *Essai* 184-91; *EI²* II.249; cf. Ibn ʿArabī, *La vie merveilleuse*]

FARQAD AL-SABAKHĪ [d. 131/748]. Otherwise known as Abū Yaʿqūb al-Baṣrī; reputed for his truthfulness. [Zabīdī 98]

FATḤ B. SAʿĪD AL-MAWṢILĪ [d. 320/932]. A great mystic from Baghdad. Known for his piety and thought to have performed miracles, such as walking on water. He was of the generation of Bishr al-Ḥāfī and Sarī al-Ṣaqaṭī. [Nabhānī II.437; *Tarīkh Baghdād* XII.381-83]

GHAZWĀN [no dates]. Perhaps Ghazwān b. ʿAtaba b. Ghazwān al-Māzinī who was one of the *Tābiʿīn*. [Zabīdī 116]

ḤABĪBA AL-ʿADAWIYYA [no dates]. A pious woman from Basra known for her devotions and constancy of prayer. [Zabīdī 138].

AL-ḤAJJĀJ B. YŪSUF AL-THAQAFĪ [d. 95/714]. Umayyad governor of Basra, infamously known for his brutal campaigns against the lawless Kharijites and, later, Ibn al-Zubayr, whom he defeated at Mecca under the reign of Caliph ʿAbd al-Malik. [Zabīdī 113; *EI*² III.39-43].

ḤUMAYD AL-ṬAWĪL AL-BAṢRĪ, ABŪ ʿUBAYDA [d. 142/759]. One of the *Tābiʿūn*. Died at 75 years old. [Zabīdī 98]

AL-ḤARTH B. ʿABD ALLĀH AL-MAKHZŪMĪ AL-MAKKĪ [d. *ca.* 70/689]. Amīr of Kufa. [Zabīdī 120]

AL-ḤASAN AL-BAṢRĪ [d. 110/728]. One of the most outstanding intellectual figures in early *kalām*, al-Ḥasan participated in the major political and philosophical debates of his time. He was considered a distant forerunner of Muʿtazilism, on certain doctrinal emphases, but was especially respected for the ascetic life he led. [Abū Nuʿaym II.131-61; Ibn Khallikān II.69-73; Dhahabī (2) I.71-2, no. 66; Nabhānī II.21; Hujwīrī 115-16; Massignon, *Essai* 174-201; Watt 64, 103-4ff; *EI*² III.254-55]

ḤASSĀN B. ABĪ SUNĀN [d. *ca.* 167/783-84]. Holy man from Basra and transmitter of information about the life of al-Ḥasan al-Baṣrī and Thābiṭ al-Bunānī. [Abū Nuʿaym III.114-20; Ibn Jawzī III.254-57]

ḤUDHAYFA B. QATĀDA AL-MARʿASHI [d. 207/822-23]. Ascetic disciple of Ibn Adham and Sufyān al-Thawrī. [Abū Nuʿaym VIII.267-71; Ibn al-Jawzī IV.242-45]

ʿIBĀDA B. ṢĀMIT [d. 34-5/654-55]. Died in Ramalah.

IBN ʿAṬĀʾ AL-RŪDHBĀRĪ, ABŪ ʿABD ALLĀH AḤMAD [d. 369/979]. Famous Shaykh from Syria who upheld religious law and the *Sunna* in every discipline and exercise. Died in Basra. [Qushayrī 51; Zabīdī 96]

IBN AL-MUBĀRAK, ʿABD ALLĀH [b. 118-81/736-97]. Born in Merv. Author of important compilation on *zuhd* (abstinence), Ibn al-Mubārak joined prophetic traditions with the moral and religious sciences and the law. He studied under Sufyān al-Thawrī and Mālik b. Anas, from whom he transmitted the *Muwaṭṭaʾ*. He travelled extensively and took part in military expeditions. [Abu Nuʿaym VIII.162-90; Ibn Khallikān III.32-4; Dhahabī (2) I.274-79, no. 260; *EI*² III.903]

IBN AL-SAMMĀK, ABŪ AL-ʿABBĀS [d. 183/799]. Ascetic and traditionist of Kufa. Lived for a time at Baghdad, where he met Caliph Harūn al-Rashīd. [Abū Nuʿaym VIII.203-17; Dhahabī (1) I.221; Ibn Jawzī III.105-5; Ibn Khallikān IV.301-2; Zabīdī 117]

IBRĀHĪM B. AḤMAD AL-KHAWWĀS, ABŪ ISḤĀQ [d. 291/903-4]. Associated with Junayd's circle. Famed for his piety and spiritual discipline, he used to wander the deserts without provisions, relying solely on the *ʿaṭā' al-tawakkul*—namely, the gift of reliance granted by God. [Abū Nuʿaym X.325-31; Ibn Jawzī IV.80-4; Jāmī 136-9; Zabīdī 285, 372; Schimmel 119]

IBRĀHĪM B. YAZĪDĪ B. AL-ḤĀRITH AL-TAYMĪ [d. 92/710-11]. Ascetic from Kufa. Followed an austere form of spiritual discipline. Al-Ḥajjāj imprisoned him and had him killed at forty years of age. [Abū Nuʿaym IV.210-19; Dhahabī (2) I.73, no. 69; Nabhānī I.384-5]

ʿĪSĀ B. YŪNUS AL-MIṢRĪ [d. 188/804]. Traditionist and ascetic from Kufa. He participated in numerous military expeditions and finally died in Syria. [Dhahabī (2) I.279-82, no. 261; cf. Ibn Jawzī IV.234-35]

JAʿFAR B. MUḤAMMAD [d. 348-959]. In Baghdad, he was a disciple of Junayd, Nurī, Ruwaym, Samnūn and Jurayrī, and an important authority on mystical tradition in his own right. [Abū Nuʿaym X.381-82; Ibn al-Mulaqqin 170-74]

JUNAYD, ABŪ AL-QĀSIM B. MUḤAMMAD [d. 298/910-11]. One of the most influential figures in early Sufism who traced his roots to Nāhavand, the ancient royal capital of the Sassanians. He learned from Sarī al-Saqaṭī and al-Hārith al-Muḥāsibī. [Abū Nuʿaym X.255-87; Sulamī 155-63; Ibn Khallikān I.373-75 *EI*[2] II.384-85]

AL-JURAYRĪ, ABŪ MUḤAMMAD AḤMAD [d. 311/923-24]. Studied under Sahl Tustarī and was one of the closest companions of Junayd, whom he succeeded in Baghdad. [Qushayrī 39-40; Sulamī 259-64; Ibn Mulaqqin 71-5]

KAʿB B. MĀTIʿ AL-HIMYĀRĪ AL-AḤBĀR [d. 32/652/3]. A Jewish-Yemeni scholar, Kaʿb embraced Islam in Syria after the death of the Prophet. When ʿUmar was caliph he travelled to Medina, where he met many Companions. He was known mostly as an authority on Judeo-Islamic traditions. [Abū Nuʿaym V.363-91, VI.3-48; Ibn Jawzī IV.175-77; Dhahabī (2) I.52, no. 33; Ibn Ḥajar (1) III.315-17, no. 7496; *EI*[2] IV.317-7]

MĀLIK B. DĪNĀR, ABŪ YAḤYĀ AL-BAṢRĪ [d. 131/748-49]. A well known learned figure and ascetic from Basra who earned his living as a copyist of the

Qur'ān; he was particularly interested in the Qur'ān's variant readings. His sayings, which had a distinctly moralistic flavour, wedded sincerity to action. [Abū Nuʿaym II.357-89; Ibn al-Mulaqqin 386-97; Hujwīrī 118-19; ʿAṭṭār 26-31; Pellat 99; *EI*² VI.266-67]

MANṢŪR B. ʿAMMĀR, ABŪ AL-SARĪ [d. *ca.* 4th century]. Considered one of the best preachers and wisest of his time. He taught that the comeliest garments were humility and piety. [Qushayrī 30; Abū Nuʿaym IX.325]

MANṢŪR B. AL-MUʿTAMAR, ABŪ ʿATĀB [d. *ca.* 132/749-50]. Transmitted several traditions of the Prophet but was reportedly opposed to writing them down, a practice considered controversial by some at the time, and advocated memorisation instead. Known also for having fasted for forty years, all during which he held night vigils. [Dhahabī (2) I.142-43, no. 135; Ibn Jawzī III.62-64; Azmi 87-8].

MASRŪQ B. AL-AJDAʿ B. MĀLIK AL-HAMDĀNĪ [d. 63/682-3]. A respected traditionist and *Tābiʿī* from Kufa who fought for ʿAlī against the Khārijites. It is said that he was 'stolen' as a young boy and later found, hence the name Masrūq. [Qushayrī 39; Zabīdī 122, 126; Azmi 56; Winter 300-1]

MAYMŪN B. MAHRĀN [d. *ca.* 117-735-36]. *Kātib* (secretary) of Caliph ʿUmar b. ʿAbd al-ʿAzīz. He was a pupil of al-Ḥasan al-Baṣrī and became a traditionist and ascetic in his own right. [Abū Nuʿaym IV.82-97]

MUʿĀDH B. JABAL AL-KHAZRAJ [d. 14/635]. The Prophet's governor in Yemen, Muʿādh was an early convert to Islam whose legal opinion was respected. [Winter 301]

MUʿĀDHA BINT ʿABD ALLĀH AL-ʿADAWIYYA [d. 83-702]. A devoutly observant woman, Muʿādha transmitted prophetic traditions from ʿAlī b. Abī Ṭālib. These traditions were written down by Yazīd al-Rashk and subsequently copied by Shuʿba. [Azmi 68]

MUʿĀWIYA B. ABĪ SUFYĀN B. ḤARB B. UMAYYA [*r.* 40-60/661-80]. The first member of the Umayya tribe to become caliph. His conflict with ʿAlī and his supporters was severe enough to cause a major rift among Muslims over the succession to the caliphate

MUḤAMMAD B. ʿALĪ B. AL-ḤUSAYN [d. 114/732-33]. Fifth *Imām* in Shiʿa tradition and widely venerated by Sufis. [Abū Nuʿaym III.180-92; Ibn Jawzī II.60-3; Dhahabī (2) I.124-25, no. 109]

MUḤAMMAD B. ʿALĪ AL-TIRMIDHĪ, ABŪ ʿABD ALLĀH [d. 285/898]. One of the most learned figures from Khurasan. Lived in Balkh, where he studied with influential Sufis. Among his teachings was that success should not be judged by quantity but by sincerity and improvement. He wrote many books, including *Kitāb al-ḥaqīqa al-adamiyya*, *Kitāb al-ʿaql wa'l-hawā*, and *Kitāb al-amthāl min al-Kitāb wa'l-Sunna* [Sulamī 217-20; Abū Nuʿaym x.233-35]

MUḤAMMAD B. BISHR [d. 203/818]. A highly respected traditionist. [Zabīdī 119]

MUḤAMMAD B. ISḤĀQ B. YASĀR AL-MADANĪ [d. *c.* 151/768]. A *mawlā* of Qays b. Mukhrama b. al-Muṭṭabib b. ʿAbd al-Munāf who transmitted traditions from Abū Salama b. ʿAbd al-Raḥmān, he also met Anas b. Mālik. He compiled a long biography of the Prophet which survived in one version thanks to Ibn Hishām. He went to Baghdad in 150 AH. [Zabīdī 131; Azmi 153]

MUḤAMMAD B. MASLAMA [d. 46/666]. A Companion, he used to write down the sayings of the Prophet. At his death, a parchment containing some traditions was found on him. [Azmi 54]

MUḤAMMAD B. WĀSIʿ AL-BAṢRĪ, ABŪ ʿABD ALLĀH [d. 123/740-41]. Ascetic and traditionist from Basra. Known especially for his humility, he reportedly refused the position of judge. [Abū Nuʿaym II.345-57; Ibn Jawzī III.190-95; Dhahabī (1) I.121]

AL-MUḤĀSIBĪ, ABŪ ʿABD ALLĀH AL-ḤĀRITH B. ASAD [d. 243/857]. A Shāfiʿī jurist—like Ghazālī, who was influenced by his thought—and a *mutakallim*. Despite his refutation of the Muʿtazilites, he was still accused by Aḥmad b. Ḥanbal of retaining some of *kalām*'s speculative tendencies. [Qushayrī 20; Watt 282]

AL-MURTAʿISH, ABŪ MUḤAMMAD ʿABD ALLĀH B. MUḤAMMAD [d. 328/939]. Murtaʿish was one of Junayd's companions in Baghdad, where he died. [Qushayrī 43; Zabīdī 97]

AL-NŪRĪ, ABŪ AL-ḤUSAYN AḤMAD B. MUḤAMMAD AL-BAGHDĀDĪ [d. 297/909]. An early figure in Sufism, Nūrī served as a model for many aspiring ascetics. His school figures among the ten branches of Sufism which Hujwīrī considered legitimate. He was a disciple of Sarī al-Saqaṭī and a companion of Junayd, who founded another, much more influential branch. He used to say, 'Sufism is neither text nor science, but ethics (*akhlāq*).' [Abū Nuʿaym x.249; Sulamī 164-9; Jāmī 78-83; Hujwīrī 162-3; Massignon 17]

AL-QĀSIM B. MUḤAMMAD B. ABĪ BAKR AL-ṢĀDIQ [d. 106/724]. Considered the most knowledgeable on ʿĀ'isha's *ḥadīths*. It is said that ʿĀ'isha, his aunt, raised him after his father died. [Zabīdī 131]

RABĪᶜ B. KHUTHAYM KUZBAYR B. ᶜĀ'IDH AL-THAWRĪ AL-KŪFĪ [d. 64/683]. A Kufan, Rabīᶜ was a *Tābiᶜī* and one of the foremost ascetics (*zuhhād*). Despite chronic illness, he was renowned for his devotional acts. [Ibn Ḥanbal 458-74; Abū Nuᶜaym II.105-18; Ibn Jawzī III.31-6; Dhahabī (2) I.57-8, no. 41]

AL-RŪDHBĀRĪ, ABŪ ᶜALĪ AḤMAD B. MUḤAMMAD [d. 322/933-34]. Mystic of Baghdad and companion of Junayd and Nūrī. He was also a disciple of Ibn al-Jallā, becoming a master in his own right in Egypt. Said to be one of the most knowledgeable and respected in his Sufi order. [Sulamī 354-60]

SAᶜD B. ABĪ WAQQĀṢ [d. 55/674-75]. One of the ten Companions of the Prophet who were promised Paradise, he remained neutral during the conflict known as *al-Fitna al-Kubra*, refusing to fight for either Muᶜāwiya or ᶜAlī. [Abū Nuᶜaym I.92-4; Ibn Jawzī I.138-41; Dhahabī (2) I.22-3, no. 9; Ibn Ḥajar (1) II.33-4, no. 3194]

SAHL B. ᶜABD ALLĀH AL-TUSTARĪ, ABŪ MUḤAMMAD [d. 282/896]. Studied with Sufyān al-Thawrī and said to have met Dhū al-Nūn in Mecca on his pilgrimage. A commentary on the Qur'an is attributed to him. His contributions to Sufism were both practical and theoretical—the latter includes his theory of revealed light. He had a reputation for strict spiritual exercises. [Abū Nuᶜaym I.189; Sulamī 206-11; Jāmī I.66-8; Nabhānī II.110]

SAMNŪN B. ḤAMZA, ABŪ AL-ḤASAN [d. 300/913]. Ascetic known for his theme of love. He knew Sarī al-Saqaṭī and was a contemporary of Junayd. He travelled to Jerusalem, where severe exposure to the elements made him intensely sensitive to the physical suffering of others. [Abū Nuᶜaym X.309-14; Sulamī 195-99; *Tarīkh Baghdād* IX.234-37]

SHADDĀD B. AWS AL-THĀBIT [d. 58/677]. Nephew of the poet Ḥassān b. Thābit. He is said to have dictated traditions of the Prophet to two Companions. [Azmi 56]

SHAᶜWĀNA [second century A.H./ninth century C.E.]. A woman of Persian origin so eloquent that many established ascetics used to attend her sermons and recitals. A pious mystic and contemporary of al-Fuḍayl b. ᶜIyāḍ (d. 187 A.H.). [Zabīdī 138]

AL-SHIBLĪ, ABŪ BAKR [d. 334/946]. Mystic from Baghdad who adopted Sufism after working as an administrator. He became known for his verses and *shaṭaḥāt* (ecstatic states). He knew Ḥallāj. [Abū Nuᶜaym X.336-75; Ibn Jawzī II.258-60; Ibn Khallikān II.273-76; Sulamī 337-48]

SUFYĀN AL-THAWRĪ [d. *ca.*161/777]. A celebrated traditionist, ascetic and jurist, al-Thawrī was extraordinarily knowledgeable in the scriptural sources of Islam, and sometimes rated even higher than Mālik b. Anas. He was one of the first to commit prophetic traditions to writing. He was also actively engaged in many theological debates and founded a *madhhab*, or legal school, that is now extinct. Often harassed by powerful figures, he was forced to flee several times. [Abū Nuʿaym VI.356-VII.143; Dhahabī (2) I.203-7, no. 198; Ibn Jawzī III.82-7; Ibn Khallikān II.386-91; Nabhānī 98; *EI*[1] VII.500-2]

SULAYMĀN B. ʿALĪ ʿABBĀS AḤMAD AL-ASHRAF [d. 142/759]. The uncle of two caliphs: al-Saffāḥ and al-Manṣūr. Died at 59 years old. [Zabīdī 98]

TAMĪM B. AWS AL-DĀRĪ, ABŪ RAQIYYA [first century A.H./seventh century C.E.]. After living in Medina, he travelled to Jerusalem and Syria after Caliph ʿUthmān's assassination (d. 36/656). [Zabīdī 117]

TAWBA B. ṢUMMA. Unidentified.

THĀBIT AL-BUNĀNĪ [d. 127/744-45]. A *Tābiʿī* from Basra and companion of Anas b. Mālik. He related a number of prophetic traditions and was known for his great piety and for reciting the Qur'ān constantly. [Abū Nuʿaym II.318-33; Nabhānī I.622-21]

ʿUJRA [no dates]. A Basran woman known for her great piety and devotions. [Zabīdī 138].

ʿULQUMA B. QAYS B. ʿABD ALLĀH AL-NAKHAʿĪ, ABŪ SHIBL [d. 62/681]. Paternal uncle of al-Aswad and ʿAbd al-Raḥmān b. Yazīd. [Sulamī 9; Zabīdī 123]

ʿUMAR B. ʿABD AL-ʿAZĪZ [d. 110/728; *r.* 99-101/717-20]. ʿUmar II became caliph in 99/717. Although his reign lasted less than two-and-a-half years, he left a deep impact on the people he ruled. He is considered far more pious and just than most of his Umayyad predecessors. His aggressive, though relatively non-sectarian, policies won him broad support from Muslims, including hitherto marginalized sects. [Masʿūdī III.192-205; Dhahabī (2) I.118-21, no. 104; Abū Nuʿaym V.253-353; Ṣafadī III.133; Hodgson I.268]

ʿUMAR B. AL-KHAṬṬĀB [d. 23/644; *r.* 13/634 to 23/644]. His conversion, at 26 years old, altered the circumstances of Muslims, who had led a clandestine existence until then during the Prophet's lifetime. He also played a key role in the election of Abū Bakr as the first caliph of Islam. Under his reign, the realm of Islam expanded to Syria, Mesopotamia, Armenia, Iran, Egypt and

North Africa—until he was assassinated. [Abū Nuʿaym I.38-55; Ibn Jawzī I.101-12; Ibn Ḥajar (2) II.518-19, no. 5736]

USĀMA [d. *ca.* 153/770]. A companion of the Prophet who transmitted a number of traditions. [Azmi 174]

ʿUTBA B. ABĀN AL-GHULĀM [d. 167/783-84]. An ascetic from Basra and disciple of Mālik b. Dīnār. Died in a military expedition [Abū Nuʿaym VI.226-38; Ibn Jawzī III.281-85; Massignon 167]

UWAYS B. ʿĀMIR AL-QARANĪ [d. 37/657]. Although Uways lived while the Prophet was alive, his obligations to his mother, it is said, prevented him from meeting the Prophet. He travelled to Kufa and was finally killed at Ṣiffīn. According to legend, the story of Uways' geographical remoteness from the Prophet was overcome by their mystical bond, on which Sufis later modelled a particular kind of mystical perception. [Abū Nuʿaym II.79-87; Nabhānī I.602-3; Hujwīrī 112-3]

WAHB B. MUNABBIH AL-YAMĀNĪ [d. 114/732-33]. A traditionist from Sanʿā who compiled many books on the lives of past prophets (a genre known as *isrā'iliyyāt*), some portions of which have been preserved in Ṭabarānī's *al-Muʿjam al-kabīr*. [Abū Nuʿaym IV.23-82; Ibn Jawzī II.164-67; Ibn Khallikān VI.35-6; Dhahabī (2) I.100-1, no. 93; Azmi 104-5]

ZULAYKHA. Wife of ʿAzīz and the woman who tried to seduce the ancient prophet Joseph. The Qur'ān takes account of Zulaykha's fervent passion for Joseph's company and, most importantly, her reckless disregard of the moral consequences. The biblical version of this story is relatively long. [Q. XII; *Genesis* 27-50; Zabīdī 96]

# BIBLIOGRAPHY

Ghazālī's *Book of Vigilance and Self-examination*

A = Ghazālī, Abū Ḥāmid Muḥammad. *Iḥyā' ʿulūm al-dīn*. Vol. 14. Cairo: Lajnat Nashr al-Thaqāfa al-Islāmiyya, 1357 AH. With marginal notes by Zayn al-Dīn al-ʿIrāqī.

B = Al-Zabīdī, Muḥammad b. Muḥammad al-Ḥusayn. *Itḥāf al-sāda al-muttaqīn bi-sharḥ Iḥyā' ʿulūm al-dīn*. Vol. 10. Cairo: Dar al-Fikr, n.d.

Other Sources

Abū Dā'ūd, Sulaymān b. al-Ashʿath. *Sunan*. Cairo, 1969.

Abū Nuʿaym Aḥmad b. ʿAbd Allāh al-Iṣbahānī. *Ḥilyat al-awliyā' wa-ṭabaqāt al-aṣfiyā'*. Cairo: Maṭbaʿat al-Saʿāda, 1933/1351.

ʿAṭṭār, Farīd al-Dīn. *Muslim Saints and Mystics*. Translated by A. J. Arberry. London: Routledge & Kegan Paul, 1966.

Azmi, Mohammad Mustafa. *Studies in Early Ḥadīth Literature*. Indianapolis: American Trust Publications, 1978.

Bauer, Hans. *Über Intention, reine Absicht und Wahrhaftigkeit. Das 37. Buch von al-Gazālī's Hauptwerk*. Translation of 'Intention, Sincerity and Truthfulness' with notes. Halle: Verlag Von Max Niemeyer, 1916.

Al-Bukhārī, Abū ʿAbd Allāh Muḥammad b. Ismāʿīl. *Saḥīḥ*. Beirut: Al-Maktaba al-Thaqāfiyya, n.d.

Al-Dhahabī (1), Shams al-Dīn. *Al-ʿIbar fī khabar man ghabar*. Ed. Basyūnī Zaghlūl. 4 vols. Beirut 1985.

Al-Dhahabī (2), Abū ʿAbd Allāh Shams al-Dīn. *Tadhkīrāt al-ḥuffāẓ*. 4 vols. Hyderabad-Daccan: Majlis Dā'irat al-Maʿārif al-ʿUthmāniyya, 1968/1388.

*Encyclopaedia of Islam*. Ed. M. Houtsama *et al.* Leiden, 1927. Second edition, ed J. H. Kramers, *et al.* Leiden, 1954-.

Al-Ghazālī, Abū Ḥāmid. *Mīzān al-aʿmāl*. Edited and introduced by Sulaymān Dunyā. Cairo: Dār al-Maʿārif bi-Miṣr, 1964.

———*Al-Munqidh min al-ḍalāl*. Beirut: Dār al-Kutub al-ʿIlmiyya, 2011.

Hodgson, Marshall G. S. *The Venture of Islam*. 3 vols. Chicago: University of Chicago Press, 1974.

Hujwīrī. *Kashf al-maḥjūb li-arbāb al-qulūb*. [French translation: Djamshid Mortazavi. *Somme spirituelle*. Paris: Sindbad, 1988.]
Ibn ʿAbd al-Barr, Yūsuf b. ʿAbd Allāh. *Al-Istīʿāb fī maʿrifat al-Aṣḥāb*. Cairo: Ed. M. al-Bijāwī, n.d.
Ibn ʿArabi, Muḥyī al-Dīn. *Al-Kawkab al-durrī fī manāqib Dhī al-Nūn al-Miṣrī*. [French translation: Roger Deladrière. *La vie merveilleuse de Dhū-l-Nūn l'Egyptien*. Paris: Sindbad, 1988.
Ibn Ḥajar al-ʿAsqalānī, Shihāb al-Dīn. *Al-Isāba fī tamyīz al-ṣaḥāba*. 4 vols. Beirut, n.d.
———. *Taqrīb al-tahdhīb*. 2 vols. Ed. ʿAbd al-Qādir ʿAṭā'. Beirut, 1993.
Ibn Ḥanbal, Aḥmad. *Kitāb al-zuhd*. Beirut: Dār al-Nahḍa al-ʿArabiyya, 1981.
Ibn Jawzī, Abū al-Faraj. *Ṣifāt al-ṣafwā*. 4 vols. Hyderabad, 1936.
Ibn Khallikān, Abū al-ʿAbbās. *Wafayāt al-aʿyān*. 8 vols. Ed. Iḥsān ʿAbbās. Beirut, n.d.
Ibn Māja, al-Qazwīnī, Abū ʿAbd Allāh Muḥammad b. Yazīd. *Sunan*. Cairo: Dār Iḥyā' al-Kutub al-ʿArabiyya, 1918/1326.
Ibn al-Mubārak, ʿAbd Allāh. *Al-Zuhd wal-raqā'iq*. N.p.: Dār al-Miʿrāj al-Dawliyya lil-Nashr, 1995.
Ibn al-Mulaqqin, ʿUmar 'Alī. *Ṭabaqāt al-awliyā'*. Beirut: Dār al-Maʿārif, 1986/1406.
Ibn Saʿd, Muḥammad b. Saʿd b. Māniʿ al-Zuhrī. *Kitāb al-ṭabaqāt al-kabīr*. 10 vols. Ed. Eduard Sachau. Leiden: E. J. Brill, 1917.
Jabre, F. *La notion de certitude selon Ghazali*, second edition. Beirut: Publications de l'Université Libanaise, 1986.
Jāmī, ʿAbd al-Raḥmān b. Aḥmad. *Nafaḥāt al-uns min ḥaḍarāt al-quds*. N.p.: Kitābfurūsh Saʿdī, 1337 AH.
Juynboll, J.H.A. *Encyclopaedia of Canonical Ḥadīth*. Leiden, The Netherlands, 2007.
Khaṭīb al-Baghdādī. *Tarīkh Baghdād*. Cairo, 1349.
Madelung, Wilferd. *The Succession to Muhammad. A Study of the Early Caliphate*. Cambridge, UK: Cambridge University Press, 2001.
Al-Makkī, Abū Ṭālib. *Qūt al-qulūb*. Cairo: Al-Mabaʿa al-Maymaniyya, 1310 AH.
Massignon, Louis. *Essai sur les origines du lexique technique de la mystique musulmane*. Paris: Librairie philosophique J. Vrin, 1954.
Masʿūdī, Abū al-Ḥasan. *Murūj al-dhahab*. 4 vols. Ed. ʿAbd al-Ḥamīd. Beirut, n.d.
Muḥāsibī, Abū ʿAbd Allāh al-Ḥārith b. Asad. *Al-Waṣāyā*. Beirut: Dār al-Kutub al-ʿIlmiyya, 1406/1986.
Muslim, Abū al-Ḥusayn Muslim b. al-Ḥajjāj al-Qushayrī al-Nīsābūrī. *Ṣaḥīḥ*. Cairo: Dār al-Ḥadīth, 1418/1997.

Al-Nabhānī, Yūsuf b. Ismāʿīl. *Jāmiʿ karāmāt al-awliyā'*. Beirut: Dār al-Fikr, 1992/1412.

Pellat, Charles. *Le milieu basrien et la formation de Jāhiz*. Paris: Adrien-Maisonneuve, 1953.

Qushayrī, Abū al-Qāsim ʿAbd al-Karīm b. Hawāzin. *Al-Risāla al-Qushayrīya fī ʿilm al-taṣṣawwuf* (n.d.: n.p., 1870 CE. [Translation: *Al-Qushayri's Epistle on Sufism. Abu'l-Qasim al-Qushayri: Al-Risālah al-qushayrīyah fī ʿilm al-tasawwuf*. Translated by Alexander D. Knysh, reviewed by Dr. Muhammad Eissa. Reading, UK: Garnet Publishing, 2007.]

Ṣafadī, Ṣalāḥ al-Dīn Khalīl b. Aybak. *Al-Wāfī bil-wafiyāt*. Ed. H. Ritter *et al.* Jamʿiyyat al-Mustashriqīn al-Almāniyya, 1962.

Samʿānī, Abū Saʿd. *Al-Ansāb*. 5 vols. Ed. al-Barūdī. Beirut, 1988.

Al-Sarrāj al-Ṭūsī, Abū Naṣr. *Lumaʿ*. Edited by Dr. ʿAbd al-Ḥalīm Maḥmūd Ṭaha and ʿAbd al-Bāqī Surūr. Cairo: Dār al-Kutub al-Ḥadītha bi-Miṣr, 1960.

Schimmel, Annemarie. *Mystical Dimensions of Islam*. Chapel Hill: The University of North Carolina Press, 1975.

Suhrawardī, Abū Ḥafs ʿUmar. *Kitāb al-ʿawārif*. Beirut: Dār al-Kitāb al-ʿArabī, 1983/1403.

Sulamī, Abū ʿAbd al-Raḥmān. *Ṭabaqāt al-ṣūfiyya*. Cairo: Maktabat al-Khānjī, 1986/1406.

Watt, Montgomery. *The Formative Period of Islamic Thought*. Oxford: Oneworld Publications, 1973, re-edited 1998.

Winter, T. J. *Al-Ghazālī: The Remembrance of Death and the Afterlife*. Cambridge: The Islamic Texts Society, 1995.

# INDEX TO QUR'ĀNIC QUOTATIONS


| SŪRA | VERSE | PAGE |
|---|---|---|
| II. *Al-Baqara* | 235 | 2, 10 |
| | 281 | 2 |
| III. *Āl ʿImrān* | 30 | 2,57 |
| | 185 | 58 |
| | 200 | 3 |
| IV. *Al-Nisā'* | 1 | 13 |
| | 94 | 10 |
| | 113 | 26 |
| VI. *Al-Anʿām* | 60 | 1 |
| VII. *Al-ʿArāf* | 194 | 22 |
| | 201 | 34 |
| X. *Yūnus* | 61 | 1 |
| XI. *Hūd* | 6 | 70 |
| XII. *Yūsuf* | 53 | 37n |
| XIII. *Al-Raʿd* | 33 | 13 |
| XVI. *Al-Naḥl* | 9 | 27 |
| | 43 | 27 |
| XVII. *Al-Isrā'* | 36 | 26 |
| XVIII. *Al-Kahf* | 49 | 2 |
| | 104 | 23 |
| XIX. *Maryam* | 98 | 76 |
| XXI. *Al-Anbiyā'* | 1–3 | 69 |
| | 47 | 2 |
| | 104 | 75 |
| XXIII. *Al-Mu'minūn* | 60 | 45 |
| | 99–100 | 7 |
| XXIV. *Al-Nūr* | 30–1 | 15n |
| | 31 | 33 |
| XXVIII. *Al-Qaṣaṣ* | 77 | 29 |
| XXIX. *Al-ʿAnkabūt* | 17 | 22 |

| SŪRA | VERSE | PAGE |
|---|---|---|
| XXXI. *Luqmān* | 19 | 15n |
| | 28 | 75 |
| XXXII. *Al-Sajda* | 12 | 7 |
| XXXIII. *Al-Aḥzāb* | 62 | 70 |
| XXXIV. *Sabā'* | 16 | 6n |
| XXXV. *Fāṭir* | 43 | 75 |
| XXXVII. *Al-Ṣāffāt* | 62 | 71 |
| XXXIX. *Al-Zumar* | 3 | 22 |
| | 47 | 57, 63 |
| XLIII. *Al-Zukhruf* | 23 | 67 |
| XLIV. *Al-Dukhkhān* | 43 | 71 |
| XLIX. *Al-Ḥujurāt* | 3 | 15n |
| | 6 | 10–11 |
| L. *Qaf* | 16 | 11 |
| | 18 | 9 |
| LI. *Al-Dhāriyāt* | 55 | 10, 68 |
| LII. *Al-Tūr* | 27 | 55 |
| LIII. *Al-Najm* | 14–16 | 6n |
| | 39 | 70 |
| LVIII. *Al-Mujādila* | 6 | 2, 38 |
| LIX. *Al-Ḥashr* | 17 | 33 |
| LXIV. *Al-Taghābun* | 9 | 8 |
| LXV. *Al-Ṭalāq* | 1 | 29 |
| LXX. *Al-Maʿārij* | 32–3 | 13 |
| LXXV. *Al-Qiyāma* | 2 | 35, 68n |
| | 19 | 27 |
| | 26 | 79n |
| | 36 | 70–1 |
| | 36–40 | 71 |
| LXXX. *ʿAbasa* | 22 | 71 |
| LXXXIII. *Al-Muṭaffifīn* | 18 | 8 |
| LXXXIX. *Al-Fajr* | 14 | 3, 85 |
| | 27 | 68 |
| | 28 | 68 |
| XCI. *Al-Shams* | 9–10 | 5 |
| XCII. *Al-Layl* | 1 | 53 |
| | 12 | 27 |
| XCVI. *Al-ʿAlaq* | 14 | 13 |
| XCVIII. *Al-Bayyina* | 8 | 16 |
| XCIX. *Al-Zalzala* | 6–8 | 2 |

# INDEX

ʿAbd Allāh b. Dā'ūd al-Hamdānī, 51
ʿAbd Allāh b. Dīnār, 16
ʿAbd Allāh b. al-Ḥasan, 62
ʿAbd Allāh b. Salām, 34
ʿAbd al-Raḥmān b. al-Aswad, 55
ʿAbd al-Wāḥid b. Zayd, 13, 19, 49–50
ablution, 6n, 40, 52, 55, 56
absent-mindedness, 7
Abū Bakr b. ʿAyyāsh, 53
Abū Bakr al-Kattānī, 48
Abū Bakr al-Muṭawwaʿī, 53
Abū Bakr al-Ṣiddīq, 26, 34
Abū Dardā', 47
Abū Dharr, 30
Abū Ḥafṣ ʿAmr b. Maslama, 14
Abū al-Ḥasan Kahmas b. al-Ḥasan, 51
Abū Ḥāshim al-Qurashī, 62
Abū Ismāʿīl, 48n
Abū Muḥammad al-Jarīrī, 48
Abū Muḥammad al-Mughāzilī, 48
Abū Mūsā al-Ashʿarī, 11, 40, 42n
Abū Muslim ʿAbd Allāh b. Thawbat al-Khawlānī, 54
Abū Nuʿaym, 46; *Book of the Ornament of God's Friends*, 66
Abū Ṭalḥa, 34, 42
accounting, 5, 6; *ḥisāb*, 4; the Prophet, 23; self-accounting, 6, 11–12, 23, 34, 36; three accountings of every activity, 22–3; see also self-examination
act, 22–3, 45; act before you are no longer able to act, 80; knowledge about the evils of deeds, 25; pause before action, 21–2, 24, 26, 27; pausing upon hesitation, 27; permissible act, 29; three accountings of every activity, 22–3; vigilance before the act, 22–8; vigilance upon the initiation of action, 28; see also pious deeds
*ādāb* (manners), 28–9
Adam, 79, 82–3
admonition, 9, 11, 14, 20, 36; for the soul, 10, 68, 80, 81
agreeing upon the conditions (*mushāraṭa*), 5–12; metaphor of trade and transaction, 7–8; *sharṭ*, 4n; a station of steadfast commitment, 4, 5
Aḥmad b. ʿAlī, 63
Aḥmad b. Ḥarb, 52
Aḥmad b. al-Rizzīn, 47
al-Aḥnaf b. Qays al-Tamīmī, 36, 43
aid, 30, 81; *nuṣra*, 2
ʿĀ'isha, 34, 55
ʿAlī b. Abī Ṭālib, 27, 54, 55
alms, 23, 42, 44
ʿĀmir b. ʿAbd Qays, 53, 54, 55
Anas b. Mālik, 35, 47
angel, 15, 41, 45–6, 83; caretaker angels, 19, 38, 49
appetite, 11
*ʿaql*, see intellect
*ʿārifūn*, see gnostics

ascetics (*zāhidūn*), 31, 52
*aṣḥāb al-yamīn*, see people of the right hand
al-Aswad b. Yazīd, 47
ʿAṭā' al-Sulamī, 63
avarice, 26

Bishr b. al-Ḥārith al-Ḥāfī, 51–2
body, 81; *ʿawra*, 8; death, 79; Hell, 8; piety, acts of, 9–10, 18; punishment, 39; relieving oneself, 29; seven members of, 8, 9; standing before God, 80; stomach, 8, 9, 39; vigilance of the perfectly truthful, 18; see also eye/sight; tongue

certainty, 4n, 21, 27, 56
Companions, 26, 41, 54, 66
companionship of good people, 20, 45, 46, 47; avoiding affiliation with the foolish and contemporaries, 60, 66–7, 77; hard to come by, 45, 60; hearing about them and imitating them, 45, 60, 66, 76
conjecture, 26, 71
conversation, 40–1; excessive speech, 8; tongue, 8, 9, 19, 58, 59

al-Dārānī, Abū Sulaymān, 64
Dā'ūd al-Ṭā'ī, 41–2, 43, 46–7, 50
David, 24
Day of Judgement, 11, 49n, 54
Day of Reckoning, 11, 34, 70, 74
Day of Religion, 11
Day of Resurrection, 21, 34, 59–60
death, 50, 55, 58, 71, 75–6; body, 79; expectation of, 16, 69, 77, 78; readiness for it, 16, 30, 51n, 69
desire, 41, 45; denying of, 39, 41; desire of this world, 24–5; *ḥirṣ*, 31; restrain of, 25
despair, 81
destiny, 27n
devotion, 44, 45, 48, 50, 53
*dhawī al-albāb*, see people of insight
Dhū al-Nūn al-Miṣrī, 16, 62–3
discipline, 2, 44; hardship, 73; soul, 10, 43n
disillusion, 7, 8
disobedience, 7, 16, 29, 37, 38, 62, 63, 83; Adam, 83; Hell, 8
distraction, 16, 18n, 19, 42, 67; from remembrance of God, 19, 58, 63; in prayer, 34, 42, 52
distress, 2, 6, 7–8, 80; root of, 24
the doubtful, 9, 25, 26, 39

eating and drinking, 30–1, 37, 43, 46–7, 50, 80; gluttony, 9; privation of, 20, 52; stomach, 8, 9, 39, 52; thirst, 15, 53; see also fasting; food
ethics, 3n
eye/sight, 8–9, 15, 47, 52, 80; gawking, 8, 78; looking at women, 8n, 39, 40, 42–3; seeing God, 46; wasteful gazing, 47; see also tears/weeping

*faḍā'il*, see supererogatory acts
faith, 70, 81; faithlessness, 73–4; traits of perfect faith, 28; as unveiling and knowledge, 26
*farā'iḍ*, see obligatory acts
Farqad al-Sabakhī, 16
fasting, 15, 40, 42, 44, 47, 55, 64; hardness of heart, 81; see also eating and drinking

# Index


Fatḥ al-Mawṣilī, 48–9
fear of God, 15, 23, 34, 35, 45, 50, 57
*fiqh*, see jurisprudence
food, 30–1; see also eating and drinking
foolishness 11, 68–9, 70, 73–4, 76; affiliation with the foolish and contemporaries, 60, 66–7, 77
forgetfulness (*ghafla*), 36, 78

Gabriel, 13
generosity, 27
*ghafla*, see forgetfulness
Ghazwān, 40
Ghufayra, 63
gnostics (*ʿārifūn*), 31, 57
God: creation of man, 71, 83; the Creator, 31, 81; God sees the hearts, 17, 21; God sees us, 13, 15, 16, 28, 69; God's grace, 2, 56; God's kindness, 70, 74–5; God's love, 62; Mercy, 36, 82; Oneness, 74; seeing God, 46; standing before God, 80; Way of God, 70, 75
gratitude, 15, 80
guidance 24, 68

Ḥabība al-ʿAdawiyya, 60–1
al-Ḥajjāj b. Yūsuf al-Thaqafī, 36
happiness, 2, 5, 7
Ḥārith b. Saʿd, 48
al-Ḥasan al-Baṣrī, 23, 34–5, 45, 46, 47, 55
Ḥassān b. Abī Sunān, 40
*ḥayā'*, see modesty; shame
heart, 56; God sees the hearts, 17, 21; God's grace, 2; hardness of heart, 81; obscured by the love of this world, 24; see also heart and vigilance
heart and vigilance: heart's knowledge of the proximity of the Lord, 15; single focus, 18–19; vigilance as a state of the heart that results from a kind of knowledge, 17; vigilance of the perfectly truthful, 17–18; see also heart; vigilance
Hell, 7, 52, 53, 64, 71; denizens of, 73, 81; disobedience, 8; escaping from 74; seven doors of, 8
Hereafter, 16, 43, 55, 70; preparation for, 74; pursuit of, 80
hope, 81
Ḥudhayfa b. Qatāda, 41
Ḥumayd al-Ṭawīl,
humility, 15, 56, 57, 82
Ḥusayn b. ʿAlī b. Abī Ṭālib, 23n
hypocrisy, 16, 70, 78

ʿIbāda b. al-Ṣāmit, 11
Iblīs, 23, 24, 58, 78–9
Ibn ʿAlā' al-Saʿdī, 64
Ibn ʿAṭā', 14
Ibn Isḥāq, Muḥammad, 55
Ibn al-Kartanī, 40
Ibn Khafīf, Abū ʿAbd Allāh, 20
Ibn al-Mubārak, ʿAbd Allāh, xvii, 13
Ibn al-Sammāk, 41–2
Ibn ʿUmar, ʿAbd Allāh, 26, 44
*ibn al-waqt*, 30
Ibrāhīm b. Adham, 28, 52
Ibrāhīm al-Taymī, 35
idleness, 8, 50, 72, 78
ignorance 23–4, 48, 60, 69, 71, 76; humility, 82
*iḥsān* (spiritual excellence), 13
insight, 3, 31, 60, 80
intellect (*ʿaql*), 5; prevailing

over passion, 11; steadfast commitment as a commercial transaction between the intellect and the soul, 5–6; weak intellect, 25
intention, 22, 23, 49
invocation, 9, 54
ʿĪsā b. Yūnus al-Miṣrī, 20
*istiqāma*, see uprightness

Jaʿfar b. Muḥammad, 56
Jesus, 26, 68, 77
Jews, 39, 71
*jihād* (striving): against the self, xvii–xviii; greater *jihād*, xviii, 3n; *ijtihād*, 16, 45; *jihād al-nafs*, 3n; *mujāhid nafsihi*, xvii, 3n; *mujāhidāt*, 60–6; *mujtahidīn*, 45; striving as way to salvation, 75; true *jihād*, xviii, 3n; 'We returned from the lesser *jihād* to the greater *jihād*', xviii, 3n
al-Junayd, Abū al-Qāsim, 15, 40, 48
al-Jurayrī, Abū Muḥammad Aḥmad, 14
jurisprudence (*fiqh*), 25; jurisprudence of religion, 25; jurisprudence of the world, 25

Kaʿb al-Aḥbār, 11–12
al-Khawwāṣ, Ibrāhīm b. Aḥmad, 65
Kariz b. Wubra, 59
knowledge, 9, 14, 5, 72; faith, 26; knowledge about the evils of deeds, 25; merit of 23–4, 26; seeking knowledge is obligatory for all Muslims, 23; vigilance and the heart 15, 17

longing, 46, 55, 65, 74, 76
love: the amorous, 31; for this world, 50, 75–7; God's love, 62
Luqmān, 11

al-Maghribī, Abū ʿUthmān, 14
Mālik b. Ḍaygham, 40
Mālik b. Dīnār, Abū Yaḥyā, 15, 35, 36
manners, see *ādāb*
Manṣūr b. ʿAmmār, 83
Manṣūr b. Ibrāhīm, 39
Manṣūr b. al-Muʿtamar, 53
Masrūq b. al-Ajdaʿ, 47, 50
Maymūn b. Mahrān, 34, 35
meekness, 8, 55
modesty (*ḥayāʾ*), 27
monk, 48, 49–50
mounting for battle, see *ribāṭ*
Muʿādh b. Jabal, 23
Muʿādha al-ʿAdawiyya, 64
*muʿāqaba*, see punishment
*muʿātaba*, see self-censure
Muʿāwiya b. Abī Sufyān, 26
Muḥammad b. ʿAbd al-ʿAzīz, 47
Muḥammad b. ʿAlī, 23
Muḥammad b. Bishr, 43
Muḥammad b. Maslama, 26
Muḥammad b. Muʿādh, 61
Muḥammad b. Wāsiʿ, 45
*muḥāsaba*, see self-examination
al-Muḥāsibī, al-Ḥārith b. Asad, 15
*mujāhada*, see renewed striving
Mujāhid, 35n
Mujammaʿ, 42–3
*murābaṭa*, steadfast commitment
*murāqaba*, see vigilance
*murīd*, see seeker
al-Murtaʿish, Abū Muḥammad, 15
*mushāraṭa*, see agreeing upon the conditions

# Index


nearness to God, 50, 77; *muqarrabūn*, 17
negligence, 7, 24, 39, 43, 68, 78
al-Nīsābūrī, Abū ʿUthmān, 14
al-Nūrī, Abū al-Ḥusayn, 19

obedience, 3, 15, 29
obligatory acts (*farā'iḍ*), 23, 29, 37
orphan, 81

Paradise, 6, 52, 53, 61–2; denizens of, 61, 73, 81; five traits to attain Paradise, 16; Gardens of Eden, 15; Gardens of Firdaws, 15; *ḥūr*, 15; longing for, 46; Lote Tree, 6; surrounded by adversities, 72
passion, 24, 26, 62, 72–3; the accomplice of blindness, 27; prevail of the intellect over passion, 11; striving against the passions, 3n
patience (*ṣabr*), 3; impatience, 73
people of insight (*dhawī al-albāb*), 3, 31
people of the right hand (*aṣḥāb al-yamīn*), 17, 21
people of secrecy, 50, 54, 56
permissibility, 29
piety, 45; *taqwā*, 27; vigilance as the best act of piety, 14; see also pious deeds
pilgrimage, 44, 50
the pious: self-examination, 35; vigilance, 17, 21–2
pious deeds, 18, 29, 74; body 9–10, 18; soul, refractory to pious acts, 10; the way to salvation, 75; see also piety
prayer, 42, 46, 54, 65–6; distraction in prayer, 34, 42, 52; hardness of heart, 81; night prayer, 41, 46n, 47, 50, 52, 53, 54, 55, 56, 60–1, 64, 81; people of secrecy, 50, 54, 56; the Prophet, 41; prostration, 46n, 50, 54, 55, 61, 62; *rakʿa*, 23–4, 47, 51, 53; rosary, 52; *ṣalāt*, 6n, 48, 52 (missing the *ṣalāt*, 44); supplication, 36, 55, 61; ways in private prayer, 83–4; see also worship
the Prophet, 26, 30, 31, 33–4, 45; accounting, 23; adherence to religion, 74; conjecture, 26; death 76; prayer, 41; self-examination, 11, 33; sitting, 28; subjugating the soul, 11, 12, 41; traits of perfect faith, 28; 'We returned from the lesser *jihād* to the greater *jihād*', xviii, 3n; 'Worship God as if you were looking at Him', 13; see also *Sunna*
prophets, 6, 71, 76, 77, 79
prudence, 11, 58
punishment (*muʿāqaba*), 37, 38, 39–43; *ʿadhāb*, 15; body, 39; eye/sight, 39, 40; sleep, 41; a station of steadfast commitment, 4, 5; stomach, 39; subjugating the soul, 41–3, 54

al-Qāsim b. Muḥammad, 55
*qibla*, 20, 28, 62
Qur'ān, 9, 35, 46, 64; recitation, 47, 53, 54, 55, 57, 59; soul, 37n

al-Rabīʿ b. Khuthaym, 51, 52
Rābiʿa al-ʿAdawiyya, 64
regret, 11, 79
religion, 25n, 74, 81; jurisprudence of religion, 25

religious scholar, 24, 25, 71
remembrance of God, 9, 30, 48, 59, 64; distraction from, 19, 58, 63
remorse, 27, 29, 33, 34, 35n, 39
renewed striving (*mujāhada*), 44–67, 72; examples from the righteous forefathers, 44–60; examples from women, 60–6; *j-h-d*, 4n; a station of steadfast commitment, 4, 5; translation of *mujāhada*, 4n
repentance, 29, 33–4, 50
resolve, 24, 43
retreat, 19
*Revival of the Religious Sciences*, 84; *Book of the Defects of the Tongue*, 9; *Book of Thankfulness*, 31
Ribāḥ al-Qaysī, 40
*ribāṭ* (mounting for battle), xvii; quasi-military concept, 3n; struggle against the self, xvii–xviii, 3n; vigilance, 3n
the righteous (*ṣāliḥūn*), 8, 55, 57–9, 60, 63–4, 77
Riḥla al-ʿĀbida, 65–6
al-Rūdhabārī, Abū ʿAlī, 20

*ṣabr*, see patience
Saʿd b. Abī Waqqāṣ, 23, 26
Ṣafwān b. Salīm, 54–5
*ṣaliḥūn*, see the righteous
Salmān al-Fārisī, 23
Samnūn b. Ḥamza, 53
Sarī al-Saqaṭī, 48
seeker (*murīd*), 25, 45, 49, 81–2
self-censure (*muʿātaba*), 37, 44, 67, 68–84; how to censure oneself, 69–82; *al-nafs al-lawwāma*, 68n; purpose of, 84; a station of steadfast commitment, 4, 5
self-examination (*muḥāsaba*), 10, 14, 15, 16, 33–8, 74; after the act, 10, 34, 36–8; before the act, 10, 34; benefits of, 3, 37; cautioning, 10; how to examine oneself, 35, 36–8; lack of, 1, 3, 34, 35; metaphor of trade and transaction, 36–8; perseverance in, 3, 38; the pious, 35; the Prophet, 11, 33; sinner, 35; a station of steadfast commitment, 4, 5; see also accounting
sexual desire, 39–40
Shaddād b. Aws, 11
shame, 21–2, 29, 41, 69, 78, 83; *ḥayā'*, 21
Shaʿwāna, 61–2, 64–5
al-Shaybānī, al-Qāsim b. Rāshid, 56
al-Shiblī, Abū Bakr, 19
*ṣiddīqūn*, see the truthful
silence, 9, 37
sin, 15, 16, 25, 37, 38, 58, 69, 79, 83
sincerity, 22, 63
sinner, 35
sitting, 28, 37
slackness, 8, 40, 57
sleep, 7, 28–9, 37, 40–1, 46, 62; privation of, 20, 51, 52, 53, 54–5; punishment for, 41
soul: admonition, 10, 68, 80, 81; body, 8; deceit and cunning, 37, 66, 79; discipline, 10, 43n; felicity of, 5; metaphor of trade and transaction, 38, 77–8; *mujāhid nafsihi*, xvii, 3n; *al-nafs al-ammāra*, 37; *al-nafs al-lawwāma*, 68n; *al-nafs al-muṭma'inna*, 68; negligence, 43, 68; our worst enemy, 68; the Prophet, 11, 12, 41; purification of, 5, 68;

# Index

Qur'ān, 37n; refractory to pious acts, 10; subjugating the soul, 11, 12, 41–3, 54, 55, 68
spiritual excellence, see *iḥsān*
steadfast commitment (*murābaṭa*), 3–4, 44; definition and translation, xvii, 3n; *jihād al-nafs*/ struggle against the self, xvii–xviii; metaphor of commercial transaction between the intellect and the soul, 5–6; *mujāhid nafsihi*, xvii, 3n; *murābiṭ*, xvii, 3n, 66; quasi-military concept, 3n; *r-b-ṭ*, xvii; stations of, 4, 5; vigilance, 3n
striving, see *jihād*
success (*tawfīq*), 2, 27; success denied by God, 36
Sufism (*taṣawwuf*), 13n, 84n; *hamm*, 18n; *ibn al-waqt*, 30
Sufyān al-Thawrī, 16, 50
al-Suhrawardī, Abū Ḥafṣ ʿUmar, 3n, 51–2
Sulaymān b. ʿAlī al-ʿUẓnī, 16
*Sunna* (way of the Prophet), 9, 46
supererogatory acts (*faḍā'il*), 10, 29, 37
support, 66n; *ta'yīd*, 2

Ṭalḥa, 41
Tamīm al-Dārī, 41
*taṣawwuf*, see Sufism
Tawba b. Ṣumma, 38
*tawfīq*, see success
tears/weeping, 17, 46, 48–9, 53, 54, 55, 56, 61, 62, 64, 65; Adam, 82–3; the source of tears is the ocean of mercy 81; weeping is rest for the heart, 63
temptation, 39, 44, 77
Thābit al-Bunānī, 48, 53
time/moment, 30, 31, 33, 72; past, present, future, 29–30; 'son of the moment', 30
al-Tirmidhī, Muḥammad b. ʿAlī, 15
tongue, 8, 9, 19; remembrance of God, 58, 59; standing before God, 80; see also conversation
Torah, 12
transgression, 13, 41; body, 9
truth, 26
the truthful (*ṣiddīqūn*), 17, 27; vigilance of the perfectly truthful, 17–21
truthfulness, 27, 36, 48
al-Tustarī, Sahl, 15

ʿUbayd Allāh al-Bajilī, 83
ʿUjra, 61
ʿUlquma b. Qays, 47
ʿUmar b. ʿAbd al-ʿAzīz, 46
ʿUmar b. al-Khaṭṭāb, 11–12, 16–17, 33, 34, 35, 42, 44
uprightness (*istiqāma*), 10, 16, 73
Usāma, 26
ʿUtba b. Abān al-Ghulām, 19, 50, 56
Uways b. ʿĀmir al-Qaranī, 50, 52

vigilance (*murāqaba*), 3, 13–32; the best act of piety, 14; definition, 15; introspection, 29; lack of, 1; merit of, 13–17; reality of, 17; a station of steadfast commitment, 4, 5; vigilance before the act, 22–8; vigilance of the perfectly truthful, 17–21; vigilance of the pious, 17, 21–2; vigilance upon the initiation of action, 28; see also heart and vigilance

Wahb b. Munabbih al-Yamānī, 42, 82
Wahīb b. al-Ward, 43
woman, 39–40; looking at, 8n, 39, 40, 42–3; *mujāhidāt*, 60–6; seducing a, 14
this world: desire of this world, 24–5; leave the world by choice, 80; love for this world, 50, 75–7
worship, 2, 45, 47, 59; levels of vigilance, 21; single focus, 18; 'Worship God as if you were looking at Him', 13; see also prayer

Yaḥyā b. Bisṭām, 61
Yaḥyā b. Zakariyyā, 19
Yūsuf, 14

*zāhidūn*, see ascetics
Zulaykhā, 14
Zumʿa, 56